"Jean-François Vernay makes the case in this book for a turn to cognitive Australian literary studies, both in Australian novels themselves and in the emergence of a 'synergistic field of cognitive-inspired Australian literary scholarship.' These are new, provocative ideas which offer unexpected ways of reading a wide range of Australian fiction from Markus Zusak to Frank Moorhouse, from Claire Coleman to Christos Tsiolkas, from Linda Jaivin to Helen Demidenko. The analyses are fully alert to the scopic and haptic pleasures books can provide, the effects of the 'neurodiversity paradigm,' the cognitive mechanisms generated by erotic themes, the interaction between mind and body in Indigenous fiction, the representation of rage in the works of 'angry gay' writers, and the major public controversy caused by Demidenko's novel."

David Carter, Emeritus Professor, FAHA,
The University of Queensland, Australia.

"The understanding of what we humans get up to with each other, as members of our species and our cultures, has been the principal aspiration of both cognitive psychology and literary studies. Until very recently, however, these two disciplines have stayed rather far apart. In this timely monograph, Jean-François Vernay describes how they are at last approaching each other in mutually beneficial ways. This book shows how fiction and imagination are together coming into the center of the neurocognitive enterprise."

Keith Oatley, Author of *Our Minds, Our Selves:*
A Brief History of Psychology.

Neurocognitive Interpretations of Australian Literature

This unique book on neurocognitive interpretations of Australian literature covers a wide range of analyses by discussing Australian Literary Studies, Aboriginal literary texts, women writers, ethnic writing, bestsellers, neurodivergence fiction, emerging as well as high-profile writers, literary hoaxes and controversies, book culture, and LGBTIQA+ authors, to name a few. It eclectically brings together a wide gamut of cognitive concepts and literary genres at the intersection of Australian literary studies and cognitive literary studies in the first single-author volume of its kind. It takes Australian Literary Studies into the age of neuroawareness and provides new pathways in contemporary criticism.

Jean-François Vernay is the author of five scholarly books, most of which are available in translation or are currently being translated: *Water from the Moon: Illusion and Reality in the Works of Australian Novelist Christopher Koch* (2007), *A Brief Take on the Australian Novel* (2016), *The Seduction of Fiction: A Plea for Putting Emotions Back into Literary Interpretation* (2016), and: *La séduction de la fiction* (2019). He has also edited several special issues of international academic journals and his 30 odd peer-reviewed articles and chapters have appeared in many countries around the world. His latest monograph, *The Rise of the Australian Neurohumanities: Conversations between Neurocognitive Research and Australian Literature*, is an edited volume also available in the Routledge Focus series.

Routledge Focus on Literature

Neo-Georgian Fiction
Re-imagining the Eighteenth Century in the Contemporary
Historical Novel
Edited by Jakub Lipski and Joanna Maciulewicz

Introduction to Digital Humanities
Enhancing Scholarship with the Use of Technology
Kathryn C. Wymer

Geomythology
How Common Stories are Related to Earth Events
Timothy J. Burbery

Re-Reading the Eighteenth-Century Novel
Studies in Reception
Jakub Lipski

Trump and Autobiography
Corporate Culture, Political Rhetoric, and Interpretation
Nicholas K. Mohlmann

Biofictions
Literary and Visual Imagination in the Age of Biotechnology
Lejla Kucukalic

Neurocognitive Interpretations of Australian Literature
Criticism in the Age of Neuroawareness
Jean-François Vernay

For more information about this series, please visit: www.routledge.
com/Routledge-Focus-on-Literature/book-series/RFLT

Neurocognitive Interpretations of Australian Literature

Criticism in the Age of Neuroawareness

Jean-François Vernay

 Routledge
Taylor & Francis Group

NEW YORK AND LONDON

First published 2022
by Routledge
605 Third Avenue, New York, NY 10158

and by Routledge
2 Park Square, Milton Park, Abingdon, Oxon OX14 4RN

Routledge is an imprint of the Taylor & Francis Group, an informa business

Library of Congress Cataloging-in-Publication Data
Names: Vernay, Jean-François, author.
Title: Neurocognitive interpretations of Australian literature:
criticism in the age of neuroawareness / Jean-François Vernay.
Description: New York: Routledge, 2021. |
Series: Routledge focus on literature |
Includes bibliographical references and index. |
Summary: "This book eclectically brings together a wide gamut of
cognitive concepts and literary genres at the intersection of
Australian literary studies and cognitive literary studies in the
first single-author volume of its kind"– Provided by publisher.
Identifiers: LCCN 2021014491 | ISBN 9780367751982 (hardback) |
ISBN 9781032078533 (paperback) | ISBN 9781003161455 (ebook)
DOI: 10.4324/9781003161455
Subjects: LCSH: Australian literature–History and criticism. |
Australian literature–Psychological aspects. |
Philosophy of mind in literature. | LCGFT: Literary criticism
Classification: LCC PR9604.6 V47 2021 | DDC 820.9/994–dc23
LC record available at https://lccn.loc.gov/2021014491

ISBN: 978-0-367-75198-2 (hbk)
ISBN: 978-1-03-207853-3 (pbk)
ISBN: 978-1-00-316145-5 (ebk)

DOI: 10.4324/9781003161455

Typeset in Times New Roman
by Newgen Publishing UK

Contents

PART III
Cognition and the Body   65

PART IV
Cognition and Emotions   93

Foreword

The approach that is taken by Jean-François Vernay in *Neurocognitive Interpretations of Australian Literature: Criticism in the Age of Neuroawareness* represents a new and original reading of Australian literature. Bringing to bear the polemics of neurohumanities, this book defamiliarizes the topography of Ozlit from grunge literature to the Demidenko affair, and from the coming-of-age novels of Christopher Koch to the Indigenous futurism of Claire G. Coleman.

There are two main ways in which Vernay's book offers neuroawareness as a source for critical insight. The first is to conceptualize the text as instigating affective responses. That books produce emotions is neither novel nor contentious, but in this book emotions are grounded as neural events. The other claim in this book is that a neuroaware criticism makes visible neurodiversity as a particular form of human difference. In earlier epochs, these were differences that might have been captured, however imperfectly, by the concept of character. Broadly speaking, neuroawareness finds in the phenomenology traced by cognitive psychology a new typology of character. According to this approach, a significant dimension of human diversity can be located in the cognitive qualities that differentiate, to take a significant example, the autism spectrum.

In Vernay's chapter on *bildungsroman* as a modality in the early novels of Christopher Koch, we encounter a concept (i.e., *bildung*) that is distinctly modern, and which cuts across the ancient ascription of difference to character. The shift signaled by the *bildungsroman* is to take the idea of character away from a gallery of human types, and to posit it as something that could *grow*. But for Vernay, the *bildungsroman* is neither an account of sociocultural adjustment, nor a repetition of decisive scenic moments in the psyche, but a dramatization of early brain plasticity and, even more daringly, a mechanism for reawakening this foundational plasticity. To state this in bald terms, for Vernay and the branch of criticism that he is advocating and modelling in this book: *reading alters the brain*, even if only in transitory ways, causing him to ask:

> In keeping with scientific discourse on brain plasticity, could readings of fiction be responsible for the transformation of self-hood in readers? In other words, is the *Bildungsroman* graced with any pedagogical value or performative effect for that matter? Would readers of *Bildungsroman*-influenced novels gain any cognitive, aesthetic or moral enrichment? And above all, do we have any reliable, efficient, and measurable ways of attesting to marked long-lasting changes in readers (namely of attesting to "the development of the reader," as Morgenstern puts it) or to literature as a moral laboratory?

Vernay does not set out to answer these questions, and one can see that in their very form they will resist the methodology of literary criticism. Instead, Vernay's chapters often take us up to this precipice and stop, thereby inscribing a neural line of limit (or horizon) to the way that we read books.

However, in the hinterland of the neural networks that glimmer beyond our signifiers, there is still work to be done, and this book begins this work in relation to Australian literature. For me, the most promising aspect of Vernay's project is in some respects its most modest, which was the making visible of ways of thinking that are at odds with hegemonic assumptions about human communicability. This is admirably displayed in the chapter on Graeme Simsion's *Rosie* series, which features the neurodivergent character Don Tillman, a professor of genetics who must prosecute his romantic ambitions through the obstacles of his ASD (Autistic Spectrum Disorder). It was once said of Lacan that he gave to psychic disorders the dignity of philosophical positions. In a similar vein one might say that the neurohumanities seek to imbue the fatality of characterological difference with the dignity of a neural disposition.

Alongside the scientistic grounding of character in neural disposition, we also have in this book a fundamental embrace of multiplicity, which takes the form of a queering of unconscious norms that habitually differentiate between normal people and those who are odd. The "odd ball" or the "queer fish" is now apprehended as simply neurodivergent and the particular modes of their thoughts seen not in terms of cognitive deficit but as, to use one of Vernay's favored terms, a "mindstyle."

The ultimate value of this book is thus the work it does in the service of neurocosmopolitanism, another coinage that resonates through this book, offering a new way to understand one another.

Tony Hughes-d'Aeth
Chair of Australian Literature
The University of Western Australia
March 2020

Acknowledgments

My warmest gratitude goes to Professor Ian Gibbins and Professor Tony Hughes-d'Aeth who have been most generous with their time and expertise. I would like to thank Professor Ian Gibbins and Professor Nicholas Jose for their thought-provoking comments on a draft of my chapters. May these thanks be extended to Gerard Hayes from the State Library of Victoria and Rocío Riestra-Camacho for helping me access resources while Melbourne was in lockdown during the COVID-19 pandemic. I would also like to pay tribute to my publisher Routledge for showing a vested interest in Australian literature, and especially Jennifer Abbot and Mitchell Manners for their warm support during the publishing journey.

Introduction
Going the Extra Scholarly Mile

Writing a book in twenty-first century Australia on neurocognitive literary interpretations of Australian fiction is likely to be still perceived as a ground-breaking venture, even two decades after cognitive literary studies started leaving their mark on Australian literary studies. Although the subtitle of my book assumes we are already living in the age of neuroawareness, it does not mean that cognitive Australian literary studies need no introduction. Being aware of a phenomenon does not necessarily imply being thoroughly informed about it.

Cognitive literary studies, at large, could be summarized as a cluster of various literary criticism-related disciplines forming a broad-based trend that draws on the findings of cognitive science to sharpen their psychological understanding of literature by exploring the cognitive processes at work in the creative minds of writers and readers. Cognitive literary studies are divided into five epistemologically related, although disparate, strains which often feed into one another: cognitive literary history (which the opening chapter typifies), evolutionary literary criticism (ranging from biocultural approaches to Darwinian literary studies), Neuro Lit Crit (a neurologizing approach to literature branching out into neuroaesthetics, which covers mainly art, aesthetics, and the brain), cognitively informed preexisting theories (encompassing cognitive poetics, cognitive rhetoric, cognitive narratology, cognitive stylistics, cognitive ecocriticism, cognitive queer studies, cognitive post-colonial studies, inter alia), and affective literary theory.

While the cognitive turn was heralded by a spate of seminal publications that started being released in the United States in the early 1990s, it would take a decade or so for this first wave of scholarship to have repercussions in Australia. While a much larger number of Australian scholars have been seeking convergence between cognitivism and the humanities at large, I will restrict the scope of this book to *cognitive* Australian literary studies, namely scholars opting for neurocognitive approaches in Australian literary studies. I will therefore exclude discussions of *Australian* cognitive literary studies, an even more inclusive category, which would comprise all Australian researchers and critics – like Kevin Brophy, Beth Spencer, or Maria Takolander – taking a vested interest in cognitive literary studies regardless of the Australian literature component.

While canvassing the field, I have observed that *cognitive* Australian literary studies seem to encounter forms of ingrained resistance, as in other parts of the world. According to Terence Cave, "cognitive methodologies and explanatory frameworks have not yet begun to inflect the common language of literary study." For him, the reluctance to embrace this cutting-edge field comes "from those who remain attached to traditional modes of literary history and criticism and from those who pursue variants of the literary theory that characterized the late twentieth-century scene" (Cave 15). A challenge to this resistance, *Neurocognitive Interpretations of Australian Literature: Criticism in the Age of Neuroawareness* attempts at charting the territory of cognitive Australian literary studies while showcasing novel neurohumanistic ways of analyzing the creative and reading processes that account for the subjectivity of literary creativity.

With this three-year project, I have gone the extra scholarly mile not only to avail myself of scientific concepts and of knowledge in human physiology, but also to ban the rhetoric of scientificity so as to avoid turning literary reception into a scientific method. I hope to have made these various cognitive-based theories more accessible to an uninitiated readership. My prime intention from the start was to make these literary interpretations palatable to the lay reader and reveal the great potential this budding scientific field can bring to invigorate the humanities.

Work Cited

Cave, Terence. *Thinking with Literature: Towards a Cognitive Criticism*. Oxford: Oxford UP, 2016.

Part I

Cognition and Literary Culture

This section introduces readers to the hitherto uncharted territory of cognitive Australian literary studies and reveals the bountiful opportunities that exist for any scholar wishing to embrace this cutting-edge perspective on Australian literature. This cognitive literary history of Australia will provide an overview of this emerging interdisciplinarity and will be followed by a close reading of Markus Zusak's bestseller. Investigating some aspects of book culture and of narratives for public consumption, my reading of *The Book Thief* at the junction of cognitive science and literary criticism offers an insight into the multifaceted organic pleasures readers derive from the seductive materiality of books.

DOI: 10.4324/9781003161455-1

1 Up for a Cha(lle)nge?[1]

A Case for Cognitive Australian Literary Studies

Introduction

Cognitive Australian literary studies could be succinctly defined as literary scholarship concerned with the examination of Australian literature from any of the five streaks of cognitive literary studies discussed in my preface, or even from a blend of any of them. The prolific years (2013–2021) have been instrumental in turning cognitive Australian literary studies from an emerging trend into an ever-expanding ripening discipline that now begs for a timely synoptic survey.

This introductory chapter maps out the cognitive literary history of scholarship discussing Australian creative writing from 2002 to 2020. After discussing the rise of the neurohumanities in Australia, I shall review the field of cognitive-inspired literary scholarship and examine why this field of critical enquiry is meeting with forms of resistance in Australian academia.

Up for a Change? The Rise of the Neurohumanities and Cognitive Australian Literary Studies in Australia

The neurohumanities define themselves as the overlapping of neuroscience and cognitive science and their application to the humanities. They have a vested interest in concepts such as cognition (be it embodied, enacted, embedded, or extended), affect with a particular stress on empathy (which is overstudied in comparison to other emotions), metaphor and other mental imagery, cognitive processes and dissonance or divergence, consciousness, patterns, and mechanisms of creativity like blending, language, mind/body dynamics, memory, attention, you name it. Neurohumanities scholars explore these areas within the remit of several academic disciplines traditionally associated with the humanities (such as literature, linguistics, philosophy, the performing and visual arts

DOI: 10.4324/9781003161455-2

and anthropology), which have all adopted the neuro prefix with much enthusiasm, thus perceiving the neuroscientific turn as a highly promising new direction. As a bridging field, the neurohumanities position themselves as the missing link between science and the humanities.[2] At the intersection of literary studies and cognitive science, literary topics such as imagination, realistic depiction, imagery and figures of speech, literary attention and comprehension, identification, the paratext, emotions, fiction reading – in short, "language, mental acts and linguistic artefacts" (Richardson and Steen 1) – are now examined under close scrutiny through the looking glass of science and being reassessed in a more accurate way, which essentially means in accordance with man's actual neurophysiology. As literary organisms, readers and writers have now gained a new status.

While dynamic neurohumanities research clusters and networks can be found all around the world, whether in Oslo through the "Literature, Cognition and Emotions" program, in Italy at the University of Catania, as well as in Dublin and the United States where salons and public talks attract captive crowds, or even in Portugal where summer schools and seminars are being scheduled for engaging students, there is hardly anything structurally organized as such in Australia, save perhaps in the more restricted field of affect studies, which has inspired a subset of cognitive literary studies. Among the latter's five main strains that fall within the scope of the neurohumanities, affective literary theory (i.e., affect studies applied to literary theory) is arguably the most dynamic and structured one in Australia. Indeed, affect studies – of which affective literary theory is a subset – have benefitted from the multifarious activities of an impressive seven-year collegial project (2011–2018) funded by the Australian Research Council. The generous grant has enabled the setting up of a Centre for the History of Emotions through five university nodes covering almost all states (South Australia, New South Wales, Victoria, Queensland, and Western Australia) along with a half-yearly refereed journal – *Emotions: History, Culture, Society* (2017–ongoing) – published under the auspices of the Society for the History of Emotions, which was founded in 2016. However, to date (June 2021), editors Katie Barclay, Andrew Lynch, and Giovanni Tarantino have only managed to run one article (see McAlister) discussing affects in Australian literary studies over the release of eight consecutive issues.[3] Yet, to be fair, Jody McAlister's article does not really engage with affect studies per se, and takes a more thematic approach to emotions in colonial romances.

A quick survey of this bibliography should conveniently give a bird's-eye view of progress made in cognitive Australian literary studies. This new vision of literature, of its artifacts and their mental processing, provides a refreshing perspective, which will bring added value to the field of Australian literary studies. As Michael Burke and Emily Troscianko advocate,

> There are many obvious ways in which the cognitive sciences – disciplines such as psychology, neuroscience, cognitive linguistics, and philosophy of the mind – have the potential to enrich literary studies. These disciplines can make substantial contributions to how literary scholars understand processes of textual creation and reception, as well as textually evoked cognition.
>
> (141)

Among the works whose profiles are particularly suited for the cognitivist study of literature, you will find:

1　Works that occasionally or frequently make *explicit* reference in their storytelling to scientific research in neuroscience, cognitive science or affect studies, like Graeme Simsion's *The Rosie Project* and *The Rosie Effect* (see Chapter 4).

2　Works that make *implicit* reference to neuroscience, cognitive science, or affect studies.

3　Works that do not make explicit reference to neuroscience, cognitive science, or affect studies, but which could be thematically conducive to this method of critical analysis. In this respect, Markus Zusak's *The Book Thief* is prime material to explore the cognitive appeal of books (see Chapter 2).

4　Works whose main topic has been the focus of research in neuroscience, cognitive science or affect studies. For instance, Asperger's syndrome in Sue Woolfe's *The Secret Cure* (2003) and Graeme Simsion's *Rosie* trilogy or obsessive compulsive disorder in Toni Jordan's *Addition* (2008).

5　Works that incorporate the mind/body tensions through literary representations of emotions, sexualities, disabilities, decay, affliction, trauma (see Chapter 6), etc.

6　Works whose genre is quintessentially cognitive like crime fiction (see Pamela Newton's book chapter discussing Peter Temple's *The Broken Shore*), neuronovels, neurodivergence fiction (see Chapter 4), and total institution fiction (for a definition of this subset, see Vernay, 2012).

7　Works that achieve some psychological complexity like, say, Peter Goldsworthy's *Three Dog Night* (2003) and virtually any novel exploring the consciousness and mindset of characters, such as the works by Peter Carey, John Coetzee, David Malouf, Patrick White, Sue Woolfe, Christopher Koch (see Chapter 3), to name a few.

8   Works and subgenres dealing conspicuously with (lack of) emotions. Let us mention dystopias feeding on fear, advocacy fiction based on rage (see Chapter 7), if not romance novels, or works by John Coetzee, Nam Le, and Peter Carey, to mention a few.

9   Works and subgenres dealing conspicuously with physicality, such as works by Christos Tsiolkas, erotic literature, pornography (see Chapter 5), grunge fiction, to mention a few.

10   Works and subgenres tapping into the unexploited possibilities of the mind – typified by Greg Egan's *Quarantine* (1992) and *Teranesia* (1999) – a theme which is most prevalent in science and speculative fiction.

11   Works whose main action is set in a neuroscientific environment like Colleen McCullough's *On, Off* (2005) or based on neural technology such as Angela Meyer's *A Superior Spectre* (2018).

12   Works of nonfiction that chronicle true accounts of neurological damage and neuroplastic recovery, like David Roland's *How I Rescued my Brain* (2014) and Sarah Brooker's *My Lucky Stroke* (2020); sobering reflexions on clinical conditions such as *Unlike the Heart: A Memoir of Brain and Mind* (2019) by Nicola Redhouse or true accounts of trauma, exemplified by Meera Anne Atkinson's *Traumata* (2018) and in Indigenous autobiographies recounting traumatic experiences (see Chapter 6).

13   Controversial works like Helen Demidenko's *The Hand That Signed the Paper* (1994; see Chapter 8) and/or authors (James McAuley and Harold Stewart, Colin Johnson, Sreten Božić, etc.) eliciting strong emotions in readers.

It goes without saying that the above list is not exhaustive. A large part of the available scholarship in the field shows that they are hardly any restrictions for academics wanting to go the extra scholarly mile by dabbing into cognitive Australian literary studies. These cutting-edge perspectives on literature and its creative minds are bound to push the boundaries and afford refreshing overtures in this long-existing field which Australian literary historiography dates back to 1856. It is not hard to see how cognitive Australian literary studies will be shedding much light on hitherto neglected aspects of Australian literature, all the while shrewdly renewing its academic approaches and discourse. A cursive review of the available research will not only give the measure of what has been accomplished so far, but it will also show the fresh insight that a cognitive perspective can bring to particular works of Australian fiction.

Rising Up to the Challenge: The Field of Cognitive-Inspired Literary Scholarship

If we are to construe reader reception as a meeting of two minds, that of the writer who produces the text and that of the reader who consumes it, then cognitive Australian literary studies will find its usefulness in analyzing any work of literature, may it be drama, poetry, autobiography, fiction, memoirs, you name it. This would go a long way towards explaining why Australian children's literature has received a lot of critical attention in this ground-breaking field, even though juvenile fiction is not particularly known for being concerned with brain-related issues.

John Stephens, from Macquarie University, is to be credited with being the first Australian scholar to have published his work when the field of cognitive Australian literary studies was at its nascent stage. His 2002 writings on textual patterning in Australian children's literature draw substantially on schema theory in relation to social cognition and show the intricacies between cognitive processes and narrative strategies. The bulk of Australian literary scholarly articles inspired by cognitive literary criticism between 2002 and 2020 fall mainly into five categories: cognitive readings of Australian literary works, creativity-focused research for which *TEXT* and *Axon* journals are the most sought-after publishing outlets, body-related investigations, brain-inspired studies, and writings informed by affect studies.

Creativity-Focused Research

Because cognitive literary studies is particularly adept at disclosing the invisible, namely not so much what lies within the subtext as what happens in the writer's and reader's brains, it makes sense that a great deal of Australian research has been focusing on how neuroscience sheds light on creativity. Unsurprisingly, the major contributors to the field are the writers straddling creative writing and scholarship. Poets Maria Takolander and Kevin Brophy, not to forget novelist Sue Woolfe and Julia Prendergast, have been spearheading Australian research in neurocreativity. For a discussion of Sue Woolfe's *The Mystery of The Cleaning Lady: A Writer Looks at Creativity and Neuroscience* (2007), see the opening chapter of *The Rise of the Australian Neurohumanities*. For now, I will only pass brief comments on Kevin Brophy's forays into the neurohumanities and Maria Takolander's vested interest in cognitive poetics.

Unlike Julia Prendergast and Sue Woolfe, Kevin Brophy's scholarly discussions of neuroscience and creativity have not bled into his praxis as a creative writer (with the exception of one poem called "Mind as Hive"), nor have these creative projects laid the foundations for theoretical musings. Both of his hats come across as separate endeavors. His major contribution in the field covers three chapters in his monograph entitled *Patterns of Creativity. Investigations into the Sources and Methods of Creativity* (2009), in which he discusses art, consciousness, and metaphors in relation to creative writing. While Kevin Brophy has paved the way for the emergence of cognitive literary theory in creative writing classes in Australia, he – very much like Maria Takolander, who has followed in his footsteps – has not established any explicit connection between his published theoretical research and his creative practice or that of his fellow Australian creative writers. Brophy's and Takolander's theoretical writings have nevertheless probed the cerebral inner workings of the writer's brain, as opposed to the following scholars who have discussed the brain representations of some Australian creative writers.

Brain-Inspired Studies

Brain-focused criticism enables Claire Fitzpatrick, Katherine Hayles, Pamela Newton, and Rachel Robertson to touch on several aspects of the typical and divergent mysterious workings of the mind (consciousness, mind power, subjective experiences, etc.). The literary experiments by Isobelle Carmody, Greg Egan, Toni Jordan, and Peter Temple triangulate the dynamics between biology, culture, and self. By entering these scholars' literary laboratory, readers will be exposed to personal accounts and literary representations of the brain–self relationship, thus making some headway in this murky area, which still largely remains a conundrum in brain science. Rachel Robertson's article on cognitive difference is textual evidence of the fruitful dialogue that disability studies and cognitive literary studies can engage through neurodivergence and of the insights the latter might yield into social injustice.

Cognitive Readings of Australian Literary Works

Margarete Rubik's article on Peter Carey's short fiction is a telling example of how to incorporate cognitive poetics into a classical literary analysis that combines close readings and a broader view of the writer's stories. Rubik explains how "Carey's consummate manipulation of cognitive schemata[4] and clashing cognitive frames [...] prevents closure and leaves the reader puzzling for an interpretation" (Rubik 169). She analyzes how Carey processes his characters based on the cognitive schemata of readers, which eventually get disrupted. His short fiction tends to climax in destabilizing images that deny readers cognitive closure.

John Stephens' and Joanne Pettitt's research is interrelated and has a strong focus on children's literature and Young Adult fiction in the light of schema theory. In "Writing *by* Children, Writing *for* Children: Schema Theory, Narrative Discourse and Ideology," Stephens elaborates on material from his book titled *Language and Ideology in Children's Fiction* (1992) and scrutinizes Anna Fienberg's schemata-driven stories. The conceptual frames that Stephens identifies as the three basic stages (orientation–complication–resolution) serve as narrative scaffolding for young readers to process knowledge more efficiently and navigate with ease through the story. The configuration of schemata subdivided into "subschemata" is somewhat reminiscent of the classic narrative sequence to be found in the morphology of fairy tales.

Within the scope of her area of expertise, Holocaust studies, Joanne Pettitt's article draws on cognitive poetics (specifically conceptual integration and schema theory) to discuss the representation and uses of silence in Markus Zusak's *The Book Thief*, and in other primary sources. She borrows from John Stephens' concept of subschemata and analyzes the prosopopoeia (i.e., the personification of death as narrator of the story) in terms of a metonymic relationship which points to "the Holocaust as a conceptual domain." Metonymy has a meaning of its own in this specific context as it comes to be defined as "a predominantly referential shift phenomenon within one cognitive domain."

Adrielle Britten's analysis of Judith Clarke's young adult fiction at the crossroads of cognitive narratology and well-being studies examines what it takes to be conducive to adolescent flourishing in the literary representations offered by *One Whole and Perfect Day* (2006) and *Night Train* (2007). Britten draws on Jaak Panksepp's research in affective neuroscience (and more specifically on his work on the SEEKING and CARE systems) as well as on Mark Turner's theory of conceptual blending discussed in *The Literary Mind* (1996) "to demonstrate how Clarke constructs [...] a cognitive map of wellbeing in which the flourishing child is shaped [...] to find flourishing ways of being when deeply grounded in nourishing relationships" (Britten 169–170).

Body-Related Investigations

In her 2007 essay, Fiona Giles fathoms the interaction and interdependence between the body and our two minds (our brain and enteric nervous system, known as the second brain) by covering various body-related

topics such as breastfeeding, oxytocin (the love or attachment hor-
mone, which would years later be reported to enhance empathy), affect,
memory, embodied cognition, and the intimacy of sex. Among multiple
sources, Giles quotes research from Sue Woolfe's *The Mystery of The
Cleaning Lady: A Writer Looks at Creativity and Neuroscience* and Beth
Spencer's doctoral dissertation: *The Body as Fiction/Fiction as a Way
of* Thinking (2006). In "A Response to Fiona Giles, Milkbrain: Writing
the Cognitive Body," Beth Spencer provides an addendum to Giles'
challenging of the age-old philosophical tradition of Cartesian dualism
and stresses the importance of acknowledging this holistic bodymind
approach.

Writings Informed by Affect Studies

Most of the essays engaging with affect studies have focused on mirror
neuron-activated empathy in relation to emotional involvement and
reader reception. On the one hand, this oft-cited emotion, defined in
multifarious ways, is explored in terms of the readers' induced empathetic response to narratives, whether the focus is on situations and
characters (see Stephens and Heister), ideological causes (see Heister),
or emotive descriptions (see Stastny). On the other hand, within the *die-
gesis* itself, empathy is also commented upon in terms of its illustration
in narratives, such as empathy between characters (see Stephens). In this
perspective, fiction is envisaged as affording a simulation and modelling
of real-life scenarios. In other words, fiction provides "proxy-situated
cognition" (Manuel De Vega qtd in Heister). Although preeminently literary in her approach, Jessica Gildersleeve flirts with cognitive readings
in *Christos Tsiolkas: The Utopian Vision* (2017), a book which seeks
to uncover the ethical and affective dimensions of Tsiolkas' œuvre by
tapping into affect theory and trauma studies. In her thorough study,
Gildersleeve investigates the far-reaching implications of the literary
presence and use of various emotions such as sadness, shame, guilt,
and disgust, as well as cognate phenomena like grief, melancholia, and
desire.

   Doctoral dissertations in this field are in a large majority studies
whose corpus covers a cluster of writers like Kumarasinghe Dissanayake
Mudiyanselage's exploration of empathy in Australian Children's
Literature or Dorothee Klein's *The Poetics and Politics of Relationality
in Contemporary Australian Aboriginal Fiction*. The latter features analyses shedding light on the novels by Bruce Pascoe, Kim Scott, Tara
June Winch, and Alexis Wright. In a similar fashion, Diana Thomas
discusses the works by five Australian women writers in *Textiles in*

Text: Synaesthesia, Metaphor and Affect in Fiction. More specifically she examines the use of metaphors in synesthetic creative writing by Jessica Anderson, Kate Grenville, Marion Halligan, Marele Day, and Anne Bartlett. By contrast, Hilmar Heister's exegesis is solely dedicated to the novels of just one Australian writer: John M. Coetzee. This is far from surprising, as the acknowledged cognitive complexity of the novelist's fictional narratives, dubbed "academic novels," combined with the prolific nature of his output are highly conducive to the elaboration of monographs and PhD theses. More generally, it is noteworthy that most of the scholarship in this field probes either affect studies (see Mudiyanselage and Heister) or creative and storytelling processes (see Klein, Spencer, and Stevens), when it does not cover both (see Thomas).

By coloring the language of Australian literary criticism with cognitive methodology or explanatory frameworks and by affording a shift of angle which reconfigures the whole field of literary studies, cognitive Australian literary studies is on its way to finding its pertinence in our increasingly brain-based society. The interpenetration of cognitive science and Australian literary studies can be construed as the logical outcome of a field eager to reinvigorate the study of Australian literature at a local and international level. However, to date, it is worth noting that the Sydney Studies in Australian literature series, which overtly nurtures this ambition, has not yet published a monograph informed by cognitive literary studies. It seems that the entrenched resistance to the cognitive turn is caused by multiple reasons, which I will now try to unpack.

The Strange Case of Cognitive Australian Literary Studies

Cognitive Australian literary studies – very much like cultural studies, which also emerged at a time of crisis in the humanities and was then disparaged in its early phase (see Hall) – could potentially be hailed as widening the scope of the literary issues that narratives generate and granting the Australian literary canon more scope and flexibility. Retrofitting literary criticism with scientifically approved concepts enables the creation of overtures whilst renewing the paraphernalia of critical tools, both of which could revitalize Australian literary studies. Cognitive Australian literary studies aims at guiding readers through the complexities underlying the creation, comprehension, and consumption of fiction while renewing the tradition of Australian literary criticism by redefining its concepts, goals, and priorities. With such daunting tasks on the literary agenda, this somewhat controversial new field was bound to meet with a great deal of resistance – if not rampant hostility – in mainstream academia. To be sure, the resistance is motivated by a few factors that need to be addressed for the path to be cleared of obstacles.

The evidence that some expected form of misoneism is already at work can hardly be gainsaid if one is to briefly analyze the journals running articles by cognitive literary scholars. A giveaway might be detected in the fact that the overwhelming majority of the essays dealing with Australian fiction has been published outside the classical leading outlets renowned for promoting Australian literary studies, with the exception of a few articles published in the *Journal of the Association for the Study of Australian Literature* such as Meg Mundell's "Crafting 'Literary Sense of Place': The Generative Work of Literary Place-Making" (2018), which discusses the role of empathy in relation to literary place-making. As to all the other essays, rather than appearing in *Australian Literary Studies*, *LINQ* (which has now been absorbed by *eTropic*), *Meanjin*, *Overland*, *Quadrant*, *Southerly*, or *Westerly*, they have been published in Australian general journals, be they discipline-specific like *Papers: Explorations into Children's Literature*, *TEXT*, *Aurealis*, and *Axon*, or multidisciplinary like *Australian Humanities Review* and *Australasian Journal of Popular Culture*. The rest of the scholarship has appeared outside of Australia in international journals (*Antipodes*, *International Research in Children's Literature*, *Media Tropes*, *New Writing: The International Journal for the Practice and Theory of Creative Writing*, and *European Journal of English Studies*) or multichapter works such as monographs and conference proceedings.

In "The Elusive Brain," the last subsection of his 2014 *New York Times* article, James Gorman comments, as follows, on the enigmatic quality of this obscure organ that underpins all cognitive mechanisms:

> No one expects the brain to yield its secrets quickly or easily. Neuroscientists are fond of deflecting hope even as they point to potential success. Science may come to understand neurons, brain regions, connections, make progress on Parkinson's. Alzheimer's or depression, and even decipher the code or codes the brain uses to send and store information. But, as any neuroscientist sooner or later cautions in discussing the prospects for breakthroughs, we are not going to "solve the brain" anytime soon – not going to explain consciousness, the self, the precise mechanisms that produce a poem.
>
> (1)

It is within the context of this budding scientific field showing great potential, yet vulnerable to neurospeculation – no matter how informed – that cognitive Australian literary scholars are submitting their material to journals.

Not only are these academics and critics treading on dangerous ground divided along party lines (the pro-CALS versus the anti-CALS), but they have to deal with a great deal of prejudice. Indeed, the credibility of cognitive literary studies has often been undermined by accusations of indulging in reductionist views, neurospeculation, epistemological carelessness, and neurobabble offering a veneer of scientificity.[5] These broadsides and negative views will form the cognitive filters through which Australian academia will consider scholarship in this field. For this specific reason, it will not be uncommon for Editors running noncognitively informed publications to reject some of the submitted contributions on the grounds that cognitive literary studies is a controversial field whose reputation has already been tarnished and which henceforth warrants no serious attention.

Identifying a piece of scholarship as unambiguously falling within the scope of cognitive Australian literary studies occasionally becomes problematic. It often ultimately boils down to a matter of personal appreciation, as there is no official yardstick to indicate how much these studies should borrow from cognitive science or discuss Australian literature to be labelled *cognitive* Australian literary criticism. Having said this, the primary sources that are listed in these academic discussions should give a fair idea of their ideological orientation and interest in Australian culture. For instance, Anthony Uhlmann's article entitled "Where Literary Studies Is, and What It Does" is no exegesis of Australian literature per se, yet it discusses cognitive poetics in relation to professing English literatures, which de facto includes Australian literature. However, his very brief discussion of cognitive poetics and his sole reference to cognitive neuroscience (the oft-cited David Comer Kidd and Emanuele Castano experiment) could be seen as too minimal for his article to be listed in my bibliography of cognitive Australian literary studies that I compiled for *The Rise of the Australian Neurohumanities*.

Giving a new direction to Australian literary criticism under the sway of cognitivism will essentially force Australianists to avail themselves of scientific concepts and of substantial knowledge of the human anatomy and physiology at large. They will also be required to take an inventory of the neurobabble, which will generate fresher outlooks on Australian literature, understood both as an archive and a practice. It easy to foresee how academics "who remain attached to traditional modes of literary history and criticism and […] those who pursue variants of the literary theory that characterized the late twentieth-century scene"

(Cave 15) will feel estranged from cognitive Australian literary studies in the face of these technicality-informed discussions.

In this particular context, scholarship in cognitive Australian literary studies is at once a brave challenge to the mainstream resistance and an invaluable contribution to neurohumanistic ways of reading into the subjectivity of literary creation.

Conclusion

Cognitive Australian literary studies should be credited for pushing the boundaries in the Australian humanities and creating sought-after overtures, which are taking contemporary Australian criticism in an exciting new direction. There is no doubt that the interdisciplinary nature of cognitive Australian literary studies will stimulate fruitful cross-disciplinary conversations and foster collaboration between faculties of arts and science. The cross-fertilization of literary studies with the mind sciences could help narrow the divide between these age-old rivalling disciplines while efficiently preventing the intellectual breathlessness that might ensue from excessive specialization. The persistent push in Australian universities for interdisciplinary necessity is highly conducive to the flourishing of this discipline, which will increase student cohorts and broaden audiences while giving graduates more versatility to their profiles.

However, no matter how brave these endeavors are, the current scholarship in cognitive Australian literary criticism comes across as fairly isolated. Nevertheless, it is gradually bridging the gap between Australian literature and cutting-edge approaches in literary reception, and it is patiently overcoming the various forms of resistance which continue to retard its progress. The organization of this emergent domain in clusters of research centers in which cognitive Australian literary critics could participate in more concerted action will certainly be a decisive factor for this field to become one of the established new directions in contemporary Australian criticism.

Notes

1 The bibliography of the scholars whose work is mentioned in passing is available in the final section of this volume, see Selective Bibliography.
2 It is noteworthy that this new conceptual approach blending humanistic and scientific inquiry is strikingly reminiscent in literary studies of countless methods of critical analysis that have more or less involved a desire to establish a literary science. I have recapitulated these literary approaches in

The Seduction of Fiction: A Plea for Putting Emotions Back into Literary Interpretation (Vernay 3–4).

3 This is largely due to the journal's multidisciplinary nature, which eclectically covers a large array of disciplines ranging from cognitive sciences and psychology, to literature, philosophy, music, art, cultural studies, history, politics, sociology, environmental humanities, religious studies, etc.

4 Cognitive schemata could be defined as "a configuration of hypotheses (schemata) that offers a coherent account for the various aspects of the text" (Rumelhart 38).

5 If cognitive literary studies are to thrive at all and avoid broadsides, it has to adhere to three heuristic guidelines which Marcus Hartner methodically spells out, including the principles of: (1) coherence (by which he means that literary "theories and concepts should [...] cohere with the tenets of established theorising on those levels"); moderation (which involves a need to stick to "established, well-corroborated theories and concepts" and to avoid "taking up highly controversial, speculative, or experimental ideas that have yet to be tried and tested"); and of autonomy (which "reminds us that the study of literature may differ significantly from many fields of research in the cognitive sciences in terms of methodologies and the aims of research") (see Hartner).

Works Cited

Brophy, Kevin. *Patterns of Creativity. Investigations into the Sources and Methods of Creativity*. Amsterdam: Rodopi, 2009.

———. "Mind as Hive." *Offshoot: Contemporary Life Writing Methodologies and Practice*. Ed. Donna Lee Brien and Quinn Eades. Crawley: U of Western Australia Publishing, 2018. 209–210.

Britten, Adrielle. "The Family and Adolescent Wellbeing: Alternative Models of Adolescent Growth in the Novels of Judith Clarke." *International Research in Children's Literature* 7.2 (2014): 165–179.

Burke, Michael, and Emily T. Troscianko. "Mind, Brain and Literature: A Dialogue on What the Humanities Might Offer the Cognitive Sciences." *Journal of Literary Semantics* 42.2 (2013): 141–148.

Cave, Terence. *Thinking with Literature: Towards a Cognitive Criticism*. Oxford: Oxford UP, 2016.

Fitzpatrick, Claire. "Neuroscience in Science Fiction: Brain Augmentation in an Increasingly Futuristic World." *Aurealis* 105 (2017): 29–32.

Giles, Fiona. "Milkbrain: Writing the Cognitive Body." *Australian Humanities Review* 43 (2007). http://australianhumanitiesreview.org/2007/12/01/milk brain-writing-the-cognitive-body/.

Gildersleeve, Jessica. *Christos Tsiolkas: The Utopian Vision*. Amherst: Cambria P, 2017.

Gorman, James. "The Brain, in Exquisite Detail." Section D, *The New York Times* 07 Jan 2014: 1.

Hall, Stuart. "The Emergence of Cultural Studies and the Crisis of the Humanities." *October* 53, Special Issue: *The Humanities as Social Technology* (1990): 11–23.

Hayles, N. Katherine. "Greg Egan's *Quarantine* and *Teranesia*: Contributions to the Millenial Reassement of Consciousness and the Cognitive Nonconscious." *Science Fiction Studies* 42.1 (2015): 56–77.

Hartner, Marcus. "Scientific Concepts in Literary Studies: Towards Criteria for the Meeting of Literature and Cognitive Science." *Cognitive Literary Science: Dialogues Between Literature and Cognition.* Ed. Michael Burke and Emily T. Troscianko. Oxford: Oxford UP, 2017. 17–34.

Heister, Hilmar. "Empathy and the Sympathetic Imagination in the Fiction of J.M. Coetzee." *Media Tropes* 4.2 (2014): 98–113.

McAlister, Jody. "'Feelings Like the Women in Books.' Declarations of Love in Australian Romance Novels, 1859–1891." *Emotions: History, Culture, Society* 2.1 (2018): 91–112.

Newton, Pamela. "Beyond the Sensation Novel: Social Crime Fiction and Qualia of the Real World." *Literature and Sensation.* Ed. Anthony Uhlmann, Helen Groth, Paul Sheehan, and Stephen McLaren. Newcastle upon Tyne: Cambridge Scholars Publishing, 2009. 34–49.

Pettitt, Joanne. "On Blends and Abstractions: Children's Literature and the Mechanisms of Holocaust Representation." *International Research in Children's Literature* 7.2 (2014): 152–164.

Richardson, Alan, and Francis F. Steen. "Literature and the Cognitive Revolution: An Introduction." *Poetics Today* 23.1 (2002): 1–8.

Robertson, Rachel. "'Driven by Tens': Obsession and Cognitive Difference in Toni Jordan's Romantic Comedy *Addition.*" *Australasian Journal of Popular Culture* 3.3 (2014): 311–320.

Rubik, Margarete. "Provocative and Unforgettable: Peter Carey's Short Fiction." *European Journal of English Studies* 9.2 (2005): 169–84.

Rumelhart, David E. "Schemata: The Building Blocks of Cognition." *Theoretical Issues in Reading Comprehension: Perspectives from Cognitive Psychology, Linguistics, Artificial Intelligence and Education.* Ed. Rand J. Spiro, Bertram C. Bruce, and William F. Brewer. Hillsdale, NJ: Lawrence Erlbaum, 1980. 33–58.

Spencer, Beth. "A Response to Fiona Giles, Milkbrain: Writing the Cognitive Body." *Australian Humanities Review* 43 (2007). http://australianhumanities review.org/2007/12/01/a-response-to-fiona-giles-milkbrain-writing-the-cognitive-body/.

Stastny, Angélique. "Settler–Indigenous Relationships and the Emotional Regime of Empathy in Australian History School Textbooks in Times of Reconciliation." *Emotion, Affective Practices, and the Past in the Present.* Ed. Laurajane Smith, Margaret Wetherell, and Gary Campbell. London/ New York: Routledge, 2018. 246–64.

Stephens, John. "Writing *by* Children, Writing *for* Children: Schema Theory, Narrative Discourse and Ideology." *Crossing the Boundaries.* Ed. Michèle

Anstey and Geoff Bull. Frenchs Forest, NSW: Pearson Education, 2002. 237–248.

———. "Affective Strategies, Emotion Schemas, and Empathic Endings: Selkie Girls and a Critical Odyssey." *Explorations into Children's Literature* 23.1 (2015): 17–33.

Takolander, Maria. "Dissanayake's 'Motherese' and Poetic Praxis: Theorising Emotion and Inarticulacy." *Axon: Creative Explorations* 4.1. Special Issue: *Poetry: Writing, Thinking, Making* (2014). www.axonjournal.com.au/issue-6/dissanayake's-'motherese'-and-poetic-praxis.

———. "After Romanticism, Psychoanalysis and Postmodernism: New Paradigms for Theorising Creativity." *TEXT: The Journal of Writing and Writing Courses* 18.2 (2014). www.textjournal.com.au/oct14/takolander.htm.

———. "A Dark/Inscrutable Workmanship: Shining a 'Scientific' Light on Emotion and Poiesis." *Axon: Creative Explorations*. Special Issue: *Capsule 1. Poetry on the Move* (2015). www.axonjournal.com.au/issue-c1/darkinscrutable-workmanship.

———. "From the 'Mad' Poet to the 'Embodied' Poet: Reconceptualising Creativity Through Cognitive Science Paradigms." *TEXT: The Journal of Writing and Writing Courses* 19.2 (2015). http://pandora.nla.gov.au/pan/10069/20160717-0026/www.textjournal.com.au/oct15/takolander.htm.

Uhlmann, Anthony. "Where Literary Studies Is, and What It Does." *Australian Literary Studies* 28.1–2 (2013): 98–110.

Vernay, Jean-François. "The Art of Penning The March Hare In: The Treatment of Insanity in Australian Total Institution Fiction." *AUMLA: Journal of the Australasian Universities Language and Literature Association* 118 (2012): 87–103.

———. *The Seduction of Fiction. A Plea for Putting Emotions Back Into Interpretation*. Trans. Carolyne Lee. New York: Palgrave Macmillan, 2016.

2 Do Judge a Book by Its Cover!

Attraction and Attachment in Markus Zusak's *The Book Thief*

Introduction

At literary conferences, most scholars would discuss fiction books analytically in terms of what their narratives convey, be it from a literary, philosophical, sociological, cultural, postcolonial, historiographic, cognitive angle, or any other theoretical approach for that matter. On these occasions, books are primarily appraised for their *cognitive* appeal. However, if we are to discuss books as objects of *aesthetic* appeal, it is crucial to make a distinction between professional readers, namely those under an obligation to read, such as scholars, and their counterparts: nonprofessional readers. For professional readers, reading is driven more by necessity than by desire and so the appeal of books will be of little or of less importance. This is why my discussion of the significance of the aesthetic appeal of books will be restricted to the nonprofessional reader epitomized by Liesel Meminger in Markus Zusak's *The Book Thief* (2005). Published in different countries with different target readerships,[1] this crossover novel not only offers an accurate literary representation of the appeal that fiction and nonfiction books exert on human beings, but it engages with the other dimensions of books which have hitherto been neglected: their perception as tactile objects, their being a source of organic pleasures, and even their nonliterary functions.

This chapter will therefore focus on the sensory laws of attraction that make books so beguiling, before examining the multifaceted pleasures associated with them. Ultimately, I will explore the emotional involvement and attachment that underpin the psychodynamics of seduction.

The Laws of Attraction: The Appeal of Books

Drawing a parallel between consumerism and interpersonal relationships to define the rules of attraction, Erich Fromm cunningly observes that

DOI: 10.4324/9781003161455-3

Our whole culture is based on the appetite for buying, on the idea of a mutually favourable exchange. Modern man's happiness consists in the thrill of looking at the shop windows, and in buying all that he can afford to buy either for cash or on instalments. He (or she) looks at people in a similar way.

(Fromm 2)

To be coveted as rewarding prizes, objects must be desirable and offer good value in return. Therefore, if books are not cognitively engaging or sought out for that purpose, they are at least expected to be aesthetically attractive.

Most contemporary anglophone publishing houses[2] that are serious about sales tend to signpost the aesthetic appeal of books with eye-catching idiosyncratic cover designs meant for scopic pleasure, luring readers into taking an interest in the contents of the books. Aligning themselves with this grabability marketing strategy,[3] book designers play on various incentive-generating emotions related to object properties such as interest, curiosity, and attraction. In this respect, Markus Zusak gives a very accurate rendition of the excitement which is sometimes felt when coming into contact with books, even though the fictitious books in question,[4] which are all meant to be published prior World War II, may not have sophisticated-looking covers like the ones generated by contemporary publishing.

As in all love-at-first-sight seduction scenarios, the visual stimulus is crucial in whetting readers' appetite to pick a book and in seducing them into making an acquisition. During one of her visits to the mayor's house where she picks up the laundry to be washed by her impoverished foster mother Rosa Hubermann, Liesel Meminger accesses the mayor's wife's stately home library. "[H]olding a tower of books against her stomach" (*The Book Thief (BT)* 145), Frau Ilsa Hermann ushers in Liesel who, at first somewhat anxiously hesitant, finally walks into the room. The eponymous protagonist's visual perception of these walls lined with colorful books instantly elicits elation, a high emotional response which could be construed as a sign of infatuation:

"Jesus, Mary ..."
She said it out loud, the words distributed into a room that was full of cold air and books. Books everywhere! Each wall was armed with overcrowded yet immaculate shelving. It was barely possible to see the paintwork. There were all different styles and sizes of lettering on the spines of the black, the red, the grey, the

every-coloured books. It was one of the most beautiful things Liesel
Meminger had ever seen.
 With wonder, she smiled.
 That such a room existed!
 Even when she tried to wipe the smile away with her forearm, she
realised instantly that it was a pointless exercise.

(*BT* 145–146)

On a certain level, this excerpt in which Liesel is impressed by the
stunning aesthetic appeal of books incidentally reflects a more contemporary trend in interior design whereby books are mainly being treated
as aesthetic objects and are therefore classified by color associations to
build chromatic libraries for stylish homes.[5] When repeatedly returning
to Ilsa Hermann's library, the book thief commits a few other crimes
through the same haptic ritual:

Liesel stood in the mayor's library with greed in her fingers and
book titles at her lips. She was confortable enough on this occasion
to run her fingers along the shelves – a short replay of her original
visit to the room – and she whispered many of the titles as she made
her way along.
 Under the Cherry Tree.
 The Tenth Lieutenant.
 Typically, many of the titles tempted her, but after a good minute
or two in the room, she settled for *A Song in the Dark*, most likely
because the book was green, and she did not yet own a book of that
colour.

(*BT* 422)

Towards the end of *The Book Thief*, Liesel is having a last feel of the
books she is about to stop stealing from the library: "She left the note
on the desk and gave the room a last goodbye, doing three laps and
running her hands over the titles" (*BT* 555). Liesel's close encounters
with this stunning library – experienced as a bimodal sensory situation
involving vision and touch – brings the reader's attention to the biblio-
philic materiality of books as well as to their almost outdated sensuality.[6]
The rest of the kinetic description from that initial scene reinforces the
attractiveness and somatosensory seduction of books encapsulated by
the girl's caress which is to be felt at the tip of her exploratory fingers:

Steadily, the room shrank, till the book thief could touch the shelves
within a few small steps. She ran the back of her hand along the

first shelf, listening to the shuffle of her fingernails gliding across the spinal cord of each book. It sounded like an instrument, or the notes of running feet. She used both hands. She raced them. One shelf against the other. And she laughed. Her voice was sprawled out, high in her throat, and when she eventually stopped and stood in the middle of the room, she spent many minutes looking from the shelves to her fingers and back again. How many books had she touched? How many had she *felt*? She walked over and did it again, this time much more slowly, with her hand facing forward, allowing the dough of her palm to feel the small hurdle of each book. It felt like magic, like beauty, as bright lines of light shone down from a chandelier. Several times she almost pulled a title from its place but didn't dare disturb them. They were too perfect.

(BT 146)

Tactile object perception features prominently in most of Liesel's interaction with Ilsa Hermann's library (*BT* 146/391/422) and her last visit is no exception: "She [...] gave the room a last goodbye, doing three laps and running her hands over the titles. As much as she hated them, she couldn't resist" (*BT* 555). Rebecca-Anne Do Rozario shrewdly observes that the Picador editions of *The Book Thief* "reproduces and celebrates the tactile nature of bibliophily within its diverse covers" (104):

> Yet, just as Liesel's response to books is based upon sensation, Picador's cover does incorporate tactile elects: splashes of glossy, embossed red that could represent paint – bearing in mind that Liesel's Papa, Hans Hubermann, works as a painter – or, just as easily, blood, to exploit the more violent connotations of death, criminality and war.
>
> (106)

In this respect, *The Book Thief* – as a tactile object – is a reflection of the narrative's preoccupation with the physicality and sensory seduction of books, which both excite curiosity and afford delight.

Not So Guilty Literary Pleasures: Excitement, Desire, and Hedonic Hotspots

In an essay entitled "Literary Pleasure," Jorge Luis Borges (1899–1986) claims that, although he was "a hospitable reader" who had experienced "the greatest literary joys" in his early days, pleasure was much harder to find in reading once he became a critic:

[…] I must confess (not without remorse and conscious of my defi-
ciency) that […] new readings do not enthrall me. Now I tend to
dispute their novelty, to translate them into schools, influences,
composites. I suspect that if they were sincere, all the critics in the
world (and even some in Buenos Aires) would say the same.

(72–73)

In other words, Borges is candidly admitting that literary pleasure has
faded in the course of his change of status from nonprofessional reader
to professional reader.[7] It therefore seems that reading for pleasure is
the prerogative of nonprofessional readers like Liesel Meminger, perhaps because – unlike professional readers – they have no specific
agenda. This is the reason why they can just "read small segments" (*BT*
231) instead of cover to cover, or even drop the book if the reading
becomes too tedious or boring, an action which will bear no consequence as nonprofessional readers are not expected to complete a set
task. Another distinction is that they would chiefly follow the so-called
"impulses of the heart" when selecting a book and simmer with anticipation until they actually get to read it.

When her foster father Hans Hubermann decides to run clandes-
tine midnight classes, which are no more than midnight-oil private
reading sessions in their basement,[8] Liesel Meminger is brimming with
eager enthusiasm: "She was going to read the book. The excitement
stood up in her" (*BT* 67); "As for the girl, there was a sudden desire to
read it that she didn't even attempt to understand. […] Whatever the
reason, her hunger to read that book was as intense as any ten-year-old
human could experience" (*BT* 68). Interest, curiosity and attraction are
desire-driven emotions which build up anticipatory pleasure, namely
"the experience of pleasure related to future activities" (see Gwenolé
Loas, Anne Verrier, and Jean-Louis Monestes), which semantically
translates into words such as "excitement," "desire," and "hunger" in
the above quotes. Anticipatory pleasure and consummatory pleasure
are two pleasure centers (also known as hedonic hotspots) integrated
in the reward system, which is part of the limbic system – the center for
emotions which also bears the nickname of "the feeling and reacting
brain." The excitement related to anticipatory pleasure is the result of
an increase in dopamine levels of the brain, a chemical which produces
a reward effect and causes seeking behavior. Provided readers like
Liesel Meminger do not suffer from anhedonia, it would cause them to
want, desire, and seek out, thus creating an urge ("sudden desire") and
appetence ("hunger to read") that is reflected by the author's choice of
apt words in *The Book Thief*.

While there is no ostensible evidence of jouissance concomitant with "consummatory pleasure [which] refers to the 'in the moment' pleasure experienced by the subject directly engaged in an enjoyable activity" (see Gwenolé Loas, Anne Verrier and Jean-Louis Monestes) in Zusak's novel, diligent readers will find trace of what Victor Nell terms "attentional absorption,"[9] which is part and parcel of concentration and which must be distinguished from "reading trance" or "entrancement." Attentional absorption is facilitated and maintained in the anticipatory pleasure phase by the increased level of dopamine, "the neurotransmitter that has been classically associated with the reinforcing effects of drugs of abuse and may have a key role in triggering the neurobiological changes associated with addiction" (Nora Volkow, Joanna Fowler, Gene-Jack Wang, James Swanson, and Frank Telang 1575). As part of the wanting system, dopamine stimulates and fuels man's striving for knowledge (also known as epistemophilia), thus reinforcing brain activity as the brain actively searches for more information. This would account for the fact that Liesel is unsurprisingly described as not being able to stop reading her unputdownable book:

> Also, there was the mayor's wife, and reading in her husband's library. It was cold in there now, colder with every visit, but still Liesel could not stay away. She would choose a handful of books and read small segments of each, until one afternoon she found one she could not put down. It was called *The Whistler.*
>
> (*BT* 231)

Alternatively, the feel-good addiction in the consummatory pleasure phase that Liesel gets from reading books could be the physiological result of "the release of endorphins, which are related to opiates and give a peaceful, euphoric bliss" (Doidge 108).

There is in *The Book Thief* a more guilty form of pleasure associated with books, and more specifically with the excitement caused by their destruction. I am alluding here to the purging Nazi "celebratory fire" (*BT* 110), historically called *Feuersprüche* ("fire oaths"), the broader symbolism of which has been analyzed by Matthew Fishburn. As we are told through the voice of the omniscient narrator, an impersonation of Death, great pleasure is being derived from destruction by fire:

> You see, people may tell you that Nazi Germany was built on anti-Semitism, a somewhat overzealous leader and a nation of hate-fed bigots, but it would have all come to nothing had the Germans not loved one particular activity – to burn. The Germans loved to burn

things. [...] They enjoyed a good book-burning all right – which gave people who were partial to books the opportunity to get their hands on certain publications that they otherwise wouldn't have.

(*BT* 90)

Even Liesel, for whom a book is nothing but "precious" (*BT* 15/118) – if not "a prize possession" (*BT* 324) – is mesmerized by the bonfire:

> Although something inside told her that this was a crime – after all, her three books were the most precious items she owned – she was compelled to see the thing lit. She couldn't help it. I guess humans like to watch a little destruction.

(*BT* 118)

After reviewing the specific organic pleasures derived from books, there remains little doubt that books are objects that have been crafted to trigger emotion-induced desire through interest and curiosity, manifesting themselves during the anticipatory stage, but also through love, which is responsible for emotional involvement and attachment during the consummatory stage.

The Psychodynamics of Bookish Seduction: Emotional Involvement and Attachment

Books, be they fiction or nonfiction, as Zusak's story makes clear, are catalysts for emotions and can crystallize as much love as hatred, whether simultaneously (thus creating ambivalence) or individually. Destroying cultural property at large is a potent symbol of an oppressive regime resorting to a combined act of hatred, terrorism, annihilation and censorship to strike an emotional blow on the targeted community. On the one hand, any bibliocaust is a clear indicator of a form of barbarism that equates the devastation of libraries (standing for the custodians of literacy and culture) with the razing of knowledge, of the cultural DNA which books epitomize, and of the collective memory encapsulated in sensitive archived information deemed to be enemy propaganda. For instance, readers are told that *The Shoulder Shrug* was condemned for portraying its Jewish main character "in a positive light" (*BT* 155). On the other hand, these fascistic book-burning demonstrations are specifically mentioned in Markus Zusak's novel as part of a larger destructive scheme: "The Germans loved to burn things. Shops, synagogues, Reichstags, houses, personal items, slain people and, of course, books" (*BT* 90). By the end of *The Book Thief*, Liesel remains the sole survivor of a Himmel Street devastated by the bombs and ends up nurturing ambivalent feelings for books, which she sees as the repositories of powerful words acting as a *pharmakon:* namely, both a remedy and a poison. This love–hate relationship sounds irrational because it is grounded in an uncontrolled and cathartic anger directed at words that do not just circulate in books. This scapegoating is made quite explicit in Liesel's last thieving of Ilsa Hermann's library, where she actually destroys a book:

> She tore a page from the book and ripped it in half.
> Then a chapter.
> Soon there was nothing but scraps of words littered between her legs and all around her. The words. Why did they have to exist? Without them, there wouldn't be any of this. Without words, the Führer was nothing. There would be no limping prisoners, no need for consolation or worldly tricks to make us feel better.
> What good were the words?
> She said it audibly now, to the orange-lit room. 'What good are the words?'
>
> (*BT* 553–554)

While discussing robotics, emotional attachment to objects, and empathy in his book entitled: *Le jour où mon robot m'aimera. Vers l'empathie artificielle,* French psychiatrist Serge Tisseron points out the uncanny resemblance, in terms of emotional involvement, between our relationship with objects and our social interaction:

> Objects contribute both to our emotional stability and to the shaping of who we are in the world. As a matter of fact, being forced to part with an object to which we are deeply attached creates an emotional tension and a malaise which are similar to those experienced when we are forced to part with someone.[10]

This emotional bond is precisely the glue responsible for her insidious attachment to books, as they become essential personal objects that Liesel cannot dispense with: "As always, one of her books was next to her" (*BT* 97).

It is clear from the way that Liesel Meminger physically interacts with books that she is emotionally attached to them. The first item she finds, entitled *The Gravedigger's Handbook,* which stands out as an eye-catching "black book with silver writing" (*BT* 66), is also described as "the girl's most precious item" (*BT* 15), even if she does not possess the literacy skills to read it. So why would she dearly hold on to it? Is it bibliophilia, bibliomania, or simply the seemingly natural emotional attachment humans have to objects? Serge Tisseron reminds us that emotional attachment to objects starts at four years of age with the "transitional object" in early childhood development identified by British psychiatrist Donald Winnicott. This prosthetic attachment peaks in adolescence with "mirror objects" allowing teenagers to construct an identity of their own choosing, distinct from the one imposed by their parents or society. Later in adulthood, it finally morphs into a new level of fetishistic attachment, when adults start accumulating objects for various reasons. People might want to assert their social status, to connect with social groups, or they might simply want to feel a sense of continuity. In addition, books can turn into repositories of memories or testimonies to key moments in people's personal lives. Readers are given an illustration of this nonliterary function when the so-called "book thief" picks up her first book in the snow – the one she happens to find by her younger brother's grave. Instantly, *The Gravedigger's Handbook* becomes the repository of Liesel's memory of that moment attesting to her brother's death: a key moment in her personal life.[11] That special connection is even clearly spelled out earlier on in the narrative:

> During the day, it was impossible to dream of her brother. [...] On her first night with the Hubbermanns, she had hidden her last link to him – *The Gravedigger's Handbook* – under the mattress, and occasionally she would pull it out and hold it. Staring at the letters on the cover and touching the print inside, she had no idea what any of it was saying. The point is, it didn't really matter what that book was about. It was what it meant that was important.
>
> (*BT* 39)

Emotional attachment, when not stimulated by the various functions that books provide or when not facilitated by the aforementioned variegated organic pleasures derived from engaging with these tactile objects, can be nourished through tactual interaction. In line with the haptic pleasure discussed in the first section of this chapter, which is also illustrated in the above quote which describes the eponymous protagonist "touching the print inside," sensory exploration in this given context serves a secondary specific physiological purpose beyond the physical exploration of objects. Research in human–object interaction has proven that direct experience with objects enhances affective responses and emotional attachment to them (see Millar and Millar, as well as Sonneveld and Schifferstein).

The Book Thief exploits a couple of narrative techniques to manifest emotional attachment through linguistically constructed literary representations. In addition to referring to books as "precious items," the choice of action verbs is crucial in conveying a sense of attachment with the help of denotative lexical clues. It is noteworthy that Liesel does not simply carry books, she clutches at them, holds them firmly, latches onto them, and so on and so forth.[12] Through the use of this specific lexical field which exudes determination, avidity, and eager possession, Markus Zusak unambiguously states that the central character has a firm grip on these items. Explicit and implicit situational giveaways will also attest to how important books are for Liesel. The scene in which Hans Hubermann uses despicable emotional blackmail to make sure that Liesel will not mention to anyone the fact that they are hiding Max Vandenburg from the Nazis is quite explicitly evocative.[13] As it happens, should the little girl blurt out their secret, the first and immediate consequence would be a Nazi-inspired terrorizing book-burning session:

> "For starters," he said, "I will take each and every one of your books – and I will burn them." It was callous. "I'll throw them in the stove, or the fireplace." He was certainly acting like a tyrant, but it was necessary. "Understand?"
> The shock made a hole in her, very neat, very precise.
> Tears welled.
>
> (*BT* 220)

Another situational clue – this time an implicit one, which at first needs to be construed from the context before the attachment phenomenon eventually gets spelt out – is to be found in this excerpt where Liesel keeps enjoying the company of books no matter how adverse the environment is. Under the sway of addiction, Liesel spends more and more time reading on the floor in Ilsa Hermann's library, despite the inhospitable cold: "Also, there was the mayor's wife, and reading in her husband's library. It was cold in there now, colder with every visit, but still Liesel could not stay away" (*BT* 231).

Conclusion

The Book Thief demonstrates through its depiction of the consumption of bookish pleasures that books are more than just mere narratives that excite the intellect through epistemophilia. They also happen to be tactile objects that bring affective and sensual gratification to readers.

Like any other object, they serve multiple purposes and can be invested with various – if not sometimes contradictory – emotions.

The scope of my discussion will not determine whether Liesel's obsession with and affective attachment to books is benign bibliophilia or pathological bibliomania. What is more likely to transpire from my reading of this engrossing novel is that Markus Zusak's outlook on books is surprisingly aligned with the findings of neurocognitive research in human–object interaction. Not so much seen as repositories of stories or as consumer goods which partake of a consumerist culture, books are depicted in *The Book Thief* as the vehicles of a sensory, affective, if not kinesic, experience that stimulates most of the reader's basic senses and elicits emotions.

Notes

1 For instance, the novel was published for young adults in the United States and for adults in Australia (see Green 26).
2 I need to specify that the scope of my analysis does not take into account the top French publishing houses, which seem to resist the marketing appeal of packaging novels with alluring front covers, although they are gradually warming up to this trend. Gallimard, Grasset, Seuil, and P.O.L. still produce in their selected series minimalistic monochrome covers with nothing more on them than the publisher's and author's names and the title. Jackets and covers are meant to encapsulate the essence of the book, and in this instance the focus seems to be on the words per se and not on their imaginative interpretations.
3

> Publishers consider the entire design of a book, including the spine (which is often the book's sole introduction to a potential consumer), the size, shape, paper texture, font, etc. "Grabability" is a key marketing concern. The book must visually leap off the shelf and "grab" the consumer's attention so that the consumer will "grab" the book.
>
> (Yampell 349)

4 With the notable exception of *Mein Kampf*, all the titles mentioned in the novel are purely fictitious. Nonetheless, Zusak went into painstaking effort to give these books a strong identity by giving them a proper description and by occasionally giving away their content through short synopses.
5 Australian architects like Wendy Lewin, John Wardle and French architect Stéphane Ghestem have used books, with or without dust jackets, in and out of bookcases or on cantilevered shelves, displaying them face out, arranging them by color, if not turning book spines out or even in.
6 Indeed, it is most likely that the haptic and scopic pleasures derived from the handling of books and from the allure of covers will soon be obscured,

if not entirely ousted, by the electronic reading devices whose lack of individuality does not seem to bother digital native readers.

7 The professional reader is not a reader who makes a job out of reading books, but a reader on a mission, someone who cannot but read a book with a set purpose. In other words, this specific goal could be a summary for a class presentation, an engagement with themes and ideas for a book review, a more in-depth analysis for the purpose of writing a doctoral dissertation, you name it. Among professional readers, you will find literary festival directors, journalists, booksellers, librarians, editors, proofreaders, teachers, literary critics, and professional writers like Borges, or simply students required to study a fiction or nonfiction work from their syllabus. See the opening chapter of Vernay, *The Seduction of Fiction*.

8 Susan Koprince contends that "Zusak alters and subverts the archetypal image of the basement, picturing it instead as a shelter, a home, and a setting in which words can provide salvation," thus departing from the "dark entity" archetype identified by French philosopher Gaston Bachelard in *The Poetics of Space* (1958). While the Hubermanns' basement does come across as a safe haven, a matrix of sorts, the dark entity specter still crops up in the narrative in the form of a fantasy reminiscent of child abuse scenarios to be found in fairytales. When Liesel meets Ilsa Hermann for the first time, she is all anxious about it: "She's going to torture me, Liesel decided. She's going to take me inside, light the fireplace and throw me in, books and all. Or she'll lock me in the basement without any food" (*BT* 145; see Koprince).

9

> This model of the nature of absorption frees the term reading trance for another use – to describe the extent to which the reader or listener has become, through the narrative, a temporary citizen of another world, has "gone away" [...]. This is undoubtedly part of the reading experience, easily distinguished from mere attentional absorption [...]. Attention holds me, but trance fills me, to varying degrees, with the wonder and flavor of alternative worlds.
>
> (Nell 77)

10

> Les objets participent à la fois à la construction de notre identité au monde et à notre stabilité psychique. D'ailleurs, être obligé de se séparer d'un objet auquel on est vivement attaché crée une tension émotionnelle et un mal-être exactement semblables à ceux qui surviennent quand on est obligé de se séparer de quelqu'un.
>
> (Tisseron 94)

11 See Tisseron, Chapter 4. According to Serge Tisseron, objects tend to fulfill four basic functions, namely servitude, testimony, complicity and partnership. See Chapter 5.

12 "She was clutching at a book" (*BT* 14); "she bent down and picked it up and held it firmly in her fingers. The book had silver writing on it" (*BT* 24);

"She latched on the closest of the books" (*BT* 129); "On the second visit, she had given permission for Liesel to pull one out and go through it, which led to another, and another, until up to half a dozen books were stuck to her, either clutched beneath her arm [...]" (*BT* 156); "Viktor Chemmel [...] snatched *The Whistler* from Liesel's grip" (*BT* 324); "She slid the book from the shelf, tucked it under her arm" (*BT* 350), etc.

13 This scene is to be paralleled with the one in which Viktor Chemmel emotionally blackmails Liesel to force her to buy *The Whistler* back, a book he values at fifty marks (*BT* 324).

Works Cited

Borges, Jorge Luis. *On Writing*. New York: Penguin, 2010.

Do Rozario, Rebecca-Anne. "Don't Steal a Book by its Cover: The Book Thief and Who Reads It." *Script & Print* 31.2 (2007, issued 2008): 104–116.

Doidge, Norman. *The Brain That Changes Itself*. Melbourne: Scribe, 2007.

Fishburn, Matthew. *Burning Books*. New York: Palgrave Macmillan, 2008.

Franklin, Ralph W., ed. *The Poems of Emily Dickinson*. Cambridge, MA: The Belknap P of Harvard UP, 1998.

Fromm, Erich. *The Art of Loving*. London: Thorsons, 1995.

Green, John. "Fighting for Their Lives." *The New York Times Book Review* 11.20 (2006): 26.

Koprince, Susan. "Words from the basement: Markus Zusak's *The Book Thief*." *Notes on Contemporary Literature* 41.1 (2011). https://go.gale.com/ps/anonymous?id=GALE%7CA255494819&sid=googleScholar&v=2.1&it=r&linkaccess=abs&issn=00294047&p=AONE&sw=w>.

Loas, Gwenolé, Anne Verrier, and Jean-Louis Monestes. "Relationship Between Anticipatory, Consummatory Anhedonia and Disorganization in Schizotypy." *BMC Psychiatry* 14 (2014): 211. http://bmcpsychiatry.biomedcentral.com/articles/10.1186/s12888-014-0211-1.

Millar, Murray G., and Karen U. Millar. "The Effects of Direct and Indirect Experience on Affective and Cognitive Responses and the Attitude–Behavior Relation." *Journal of Experimental Social Psychology* 32 (1996): 561–579.

Nell, Victor. *Lost in a Book: The Psychology of Reading for Pleasure*. London/New Haven: Yale UP, 1988.

Sonneveld, Marieke H., and Hendrik N. J Schifferstein. "The Tactual Experience of Objects." *Product Experience*. Ed. Hendrik N. J. Schifferstein and Paul Hekkert. Amsterdam: Elsevier, 2008. 41–67.

Tisseron, Serge. *Le jour où mon robot m'aimera. Vers l'empathie artificielle*. Paris: Albin Michel, 2015.

Vernay, Jean-François. *The Seduction of Fiction. A Plea for Putting Emotions Back Into Interpretation*. Trans. Carolyne Lee. New York: Palgrave Macmillan, 2016.

Volkow, Nora D., Joanna S. Fowler, Gene-Jack Wang, James M. Swanson, and Frank Telang. "Dopamine in Drug Abuse and Addiction: Results of Imaging Studies and Treatment Implications." *Archives of Neurology* 64.11 (2007): 1575–1579. https://jamanetwork.com/journals/jamaneurology/fullarticle/794743.

Yampell, Cat. "Judging a Book by Its Cover: Publishing Trends in Young Adult Literature." *The Lion and the Unicorn* 29.3 (2005): 348–372.

Zusak, Markus. *The Book Thief.* Sydney: Picador, 2005 [2013].

Part II

Cognition and the Mind

This second section invites us to rethink Christopher Koch's *Bildungsroman*-influenced novels from a cognitive perspective, giving us a chance to reflect on reader response and on the potential persuasive power literature has on the minds of neurotypical readers. The companion essay pays homage to neurodiversity – and more specifically to high-functioning Autism Spectrum Disorder – through the literary representations of Graeme Simsion's bestselling empowering fiction: the *Rosie* trilogy. It examines how the endearing portrayal of a neurodivergent mind style, albeit depicted from an outsider, translates into a unique literary style and fights the stigmatizing canon of normocentrism.

DOI: 10.4324/9781003161455-4

3 Gazing Inward and Outward

(Trans)Formation in C.J. Koch's *Bildungsroman* Protagonists and Readers

Introduction

It is not uncommon for young writers to bid farewell to their youth by modelling their first novels on *Bildungsromane*; hence the fact that debut and early novels by Australian writers often relate the story of a character whose experiences are largely modelled on their author's youth. In these growing-older-and-wiser novels, the exploitation of the adolescent theme is often allied with a cluster of closely related concerns such as growth, identity, progress, and transformation. This chapter examines Christopher Koch's four *Bildungsroman*-influenced novels – *The Boys in the Island* (1958), *Across the Sea Wall* (1965), *The Doubleman* (1985), and *Lost Voices* (2012), which constitute half of his fictional output.

The highlighting of key characteristics of the genre will demonstrate that a strong *Bildungsroman* streak pervades Koch's four aforementioned novels. My critical investigation of transformation both in the protagonists and in readers will enable me to assess if Karl Morgenstern's thesis, which contends that formation novels are impacting their aesthetic subjects as much as their readers, still stands in the light of recent discussions in cognitive literary theory.

Christopher Koch's *Bildungsroman*-Inspired Novels

While Christopher Koch fully embraced the *Bildungsroman* tradition with *The Boys in the Island*, his debut novel which fits squarely into the subgenre, it is noticeable that he was less obviously committed to the "formation novel" in *Across the Sea Wall*, *The Doubleman*, and *Lost Voices* – to the point that "*Bildungsroman*-inspired" would be a better description. Originally coined by Professor Karl Morgenstern in 1809, the term *Bildungsroman* was only developed into a new genre in his 1819 lecture, in which he opposed the epic to the novel. This label

DOI: 10.4324/9781003161455-5

inspired from the reading of Goethe's *Wilhelm Meister's Apprenticeship* (1795) was initially used for narratives based on the experiences of a youthful – though generally biophysically mature – straight male protagonist. After going through a process of transformation, he becomes aware of certain realities at the end of his illusory quest. Developmental novels of this kind often explore psycho-emotional changes and moral growth, perceived as some form of movement towards completeness, or maturation into adulthood.

The aesthetic subjects of Koch's formation novels harbor illusions that for the most part rest on anything that would elevate them, such as hope, ideals, high expectations, or ambitious goals which can hardly ever be met. Francis is caught up in his fantasies of belonging to an imaginary place; Robert wishes to be given a new lease on life by turning away from his unexciting routine; Richard wants to have a successful acting career at a time when he is eking out a living from minor performances, while Hugh is an aspiring artist secretly hoping to ultimately succeed at becoming a painter while being employed as a book illustrator. They all anticipate the arrival of an event which will upset their habitual way of life – some revelation which will take them beyond the ordinary. Their expectations come as a result of loneliness, motionlessness, and routine, all of which have put the characters in a state of boredom.

The call for otherness is also a response to boredom and translates into the need for a change of setting with the eager search for an actual and/or imaginary location. In *The Boys in the Island* and *The Doubleman*, the unrewarding here and now is challenged by a seductive fantasied otherness – referred to as "Otherland" and "Otherworld" – whose charms and strength lie in the unprovable quality of its existence. In *Across the Sea Wall*, India epitomizes for Robert O'Brien a dreamed place of beguiling exoticism. In *Lost Voices* (*LV*), the call for otherness also insidiously flavors the narrative. Hugh Dixon "half-believed love might be found in such a house: behind those glowing windows, in that last spellbound suburb where an unknown land waited behind the hills" (*LV* 310).

Journeys – whether on passenger-liners or on foot, by car, bicycle, or plane – allow Koch's characters to break the mold and provoke change by emancipating themselves from the grip of their families; even though family relations are, by and large, underrepresented, or scantly depicted in Koch's *Bildungsroman*-inspired novels. Questing implies both geographical movement and a change of environment in the form of a physical or psychological escape, deriving from the claustrophobic suffocation generated by confinement or entrapment. The dynamics of freedom and constriction are pervasive in Koch's work and square well with a shrewd observation by the French psychoanalyst Françoise Dolto, who has noted that in education novels, initiation cannot occur without some form of displacement. She observes that some form of uprooting or confinement is responsible for triggering the liberating crisis, which in turn leads to the place of initiation (Dolto 56).

Each initiatory step in *The Boys in the Island* and *The Doubleman* drags the protagonists out of their illusions by fits and starts and brings them to opt for a less naive conception of life, thus experiencing a transition from innocence to experience. Nowhere is this process more clearly revealed than in *The Boys in the Island*, when readers become aware of what anthropologist Arnold van Gennep identifies as the liminal stage. This phase includes a series of rites of passage (the discovery of sexuality, the boozy excursions and parties, the racing car, the first kiss with Heather Miles) construed as acts of transgression that enable the young Tasmanian Francis to make headway in the adult world. In *Lost Voices*, Hugh's rites of passage have been omitted from the narrative on the grounds that Hugh is giving us

> a memoir, rather than an autobiography. [...] The reader is thus spared details of other youthful friendships, [the narrator's] time at Art School, and [his] first erotic adventures with girls: exchanges, like so many in the 1950s, which led to much sensual pleasure and moist frustration, and usually fell short of consummation.
>
> (*LV* 293)

Added to these key features is the central character's transformation process, which is the driving force behind these growing-older-and-wiser stories. In most cases, epiphany, disillusion and loss lie beneath the brittle surface of the ontological journeys of Koch's characters, functioning as pivotal elements in their transformation.

Gazing Inward: Transformation in the *Bildungsroman* Protagonists

In a seminal text entitled "On the nature of the *Bildungsroman*," Karl Morgenstern argues that the term *Bildung* (or formation) refers both to the central character and to the reader:

> We may call a novel a *Bildungsroman* first and foremost on account of its content, because it represents the development of the hero in its beginning and progress to a certain stage of completion, but

also, second, because this depiction promotes the development of
the reader to a greater extent than any other kind of novel.

(Morgenstern 654–655)

Following this definition, the genre itself has classically been thought
of as gazing both inward and outward.[1] The "gazing inward" phrase
implies that the developmental novels of the *Bildungsroman* tradition
are conducive to the transformation of its central character.

It cannot be denied that Koch's *Bildungsroman* protagonists lose their
illusions and gain a sense of maturity through epiphanies that occur at
various stages of their epic adventures. These *Bildungsroman* protagonists
are prompted to reread in a new light the string of events they have gone
through. Epiphanies occur stylistically through parallax, which sheds
light on new information allowing the character, and consequently the
readers themselves, to suddenly attain clarity of vision. Slavoj Žižek
defines parallax as "the apparent displacement of an object (the shift of
its position against a background) caused by a change in observational
position that provides a new line of sight" (Žižek 17). Traditionally placed
at the end of narratives, as in *The Boys in the Island*, but nonetheless at the
core of stories, epiphanies provoke an epistemological shift in perspective.
In Koch's debut novel, Francis Cullen realizes that life is no game, but
quite the reverse, after Shane Noonan's suicide and George's accidental
death. It might be noted that as part of the requirements of the novel
genre, and all the more so with respect to the *Bildungsroman* tradition,
well-rounded protagonists ought to grow, which means that in terms of
strategic intent Koch had no choice but to introduce epiphanies and epistemological shifts for his central characters to acquire the sheen of well-
developed characters.

After their enchanting interlude, insight develops, challenging the
characters' simplistic vision of life until they adopt a more critical outlook. Koch's *bildungsroman* characters are often disillusioned by their
first-hand experiences, which systematically defeat their high adolescent
expectations of profound social relationships, enhanced personal identity, as well as of personal growth and development. Their disillusion-
ment ranges from unhappy love affairs and disappointing friendships,
or failure to start a new life, to the disintegration of dreams they held
dear. Not to put too fine a point on it, Koch's novels are no narratives
of resistance in which the central characters would come to some form
of empowerment or self-actualization in the final stage of their rites of
passage. In actual fact, Koch follows the archetypal pattern of adolescent literature that "initially appears to empower teenagers," when

in actual fact "empowerment proves to be something of an illusion in many novels because so frequently, teenaged characters demonstrate to teen readers that the only true form of empowerment comes from growing up and leaving adolescence behind" (Trites 1).

Reality in Koch's *Bildungsroman*-inspired narratives often comes across as a bitter pill to swallow; indeed, the characters often experience a painful and lingering sense of ontological loss after their sudden epiphanies. *The Boys in the Island*, for example, classically ends with the Wordsworthian loss-of-innocence motif added to the nostalgic sense of a past golden age, which Francis will have to renounce in order to adapt to the adult community. In keeping with this Judeo-Christian ideology, which links the loss of innocence to the acquisition of knowledge, growing up is seen as a matter of accepting the burden of responsibilities and distinguishing good from evil.

Bildungsromane, which roughly translates as "formation novels," go *beyond* the simple idea of formation, as they imply a *trans*-formation in the protagonist at some stage through knowledge and insight, which are bound to be the logical outcome of the character's trials, and provide evidence of self-transformation. While the observant reader will surmise that Francis has rounded off his education by the end of his adventures, Robert's transformation is announced from the outset. Whereas it takes an outsider to point out the transformation that occurs in Koch's first two novels, it is the central character himself who acknowledges the change in *The Doubleman*. As to *Lost Voices*, the sudden shift of interest to Robert Wall's fate in the third section deprives readers of detailed evidence of Hugh's transformed self.

The transformation comes through the epistemological maturation of the young characters, whose ontological journeys become allegorical of their cognitive and emotional development. Of *Across the Sea Wall*, Koch once stated that he "wanted to put a man, again of rather ordinary nature, into a journey which would pull him inside out" (qtd in Hulse 20). By "charting inward journeys" (*Crossing the Gap (CG)* 152), the *Bildungsroman* symbolically segues into a Socratic quest in which an arduous geographical search stands as a metaphor for the inner spiritual journey. The male protagonist's separation from his birthplace epitomizes a departure from his earlier self and initiates an encounter with otherness that marks the return to the new-found strengthened self. This three-stage pattern aligns with the ontological theory propounded by French philosopher Daniel Sibony in *Entre-deux. L'origine en partage.* Put simply, an origin only materializes when it is lost. It is only a starting-point, which it is necessary to leave in order to possess.

Gazing Outward: Narrative Persuasion and Transformation in Readers

Karl Morgenstern's assumption will now be examined in the light of cognitive literary theory despite the fact that he does not specify in his seminal article why and how *Bildungsromane* have a greater impact on readers than any other literary genres. A quick foray into this recent field will determine if recent research in psychology and neuroscience supports Morgenstern's thesis that formation novels also possess the ability to transform readers through intellectual, aesthetic and moral enrichment:

> The kind of formation [*Bildung*] that the novel, as we saw, is supposed to both depict and confer will either occupy itself with one of the many aspects of man – his intellectual, moral, or aesthetic sides, each conceived either as general or in regard to particular purposes – or call on the community of human powers and seek to harmonically stimulate and form them.
>
> (Morgenstern 655)

By examining literature's transformative potential, I will not dwell on the sensational experience of reading and its rather short-lived bodily transformations generated by embodied cognition and sensorimotor resonance. Rather, I am interested in discussing the mid-term, if not long-term cognitive, psychological, and epistemological transformations of fiction-reading upon the self.

The question is basically to know if readers would profoundly be changed by these life-like literary representations, or at least by the protagonists' disenchanted tone at the term of their juvenile adventures. In keeping with scientific discourse on brain plasticity, could readings of fiction be responsible for the transformation of selfhood in readers? In other words, is the *Bildungsroman* graced with any pedagogical value or performative effect for that matter? Would readers of *Bildungsroman*-influenced novels gain any cognitive, aesthetic, or moral enrichment? And above all, do we have any reliable, efficient, and measurable ways of attesting to marked long-lasting changes in readers (namely of attesting to "the development of the reader," as Morgenstern puts it) or to literature as a moral laboratory?

It is a commonly accepted fact that fiction reading is transformed by the self,[2] but cognitive literary studies are now bringing evidence that the reverse also holds true. Terence Cave reminds us that literature "can be shown to promote deviance, crime, violence" (140) and "can bring about a form of psychological release (catharsis) and restore the balance of emotions" (141). Scientific and empirical research on the psychological, phenomenological, and experiential dimensions of story reception has provided over the last two decades piecemeal evidence attesting to fictional narrative impact on readers in a number of domains such as identity, personality, beliefs, empathy, psychological processes, brain connectivity and function, morality, to mention a few.[3] It goes without saying that the readers' degree of immersion is a decisive factor in the influence these literary texts might have over them.[4] In addition, performativity (which posits that, beyond its representational role of depicting real life, language can also directly impact reality by commanding it) has recently been associated with the *Bildungsroman* tradition (Boes 2012: 34),[5] thereby endorsing the transformative power of fiction, fictional narrative impact, and the fact that consuming fiction entails transformations of selfhood in readers.

In *Literary Conceptualizations of Growth: Metaphors and Cognition in Adolescent Literature*, Roberta Trites investigates through cognitive linguistics "how metaphors of growth influence scholarly conceptualizations of adolescence and adolescent literature" (Trites 124) and draws on the work of George Lakoff and Mark Johnson, who have persuasively argued that metaphors consciously and unconsciously structure the life experiences of individuals. In their opinions, "metaphors that are outside our conventional conceptual system, metaphors that are imaginative and creative [...] are capable of giving us a new understanding of our experience" (Lakoff and Johnson 139).[6] In this respect, Koch's new scripted[7] metaphor of growth, which he created in *The Boys in the Island* (*BI*) through olfactory associations and by symbolically opposing the malleability of childhood to the rigid steeled or molded character inherent to adulthood, is bound to have a conscious or an unconscious impact on the minds of professional and non professional readers alike:

> You are a fool, Lad said, because you went on listening to the story of childhood. Others forget it; but you would not. That is why you are a fool. It's a story whose end doesn't arrive: we lose it. Into the paper-sweet smell of Everything comes the tang of enemy iron.
>
> (*BI* 196)

Earlier on, Koch has subtly associated childhood with paper and adulthood with iron through tactile metaphors stressing texture. Koch refers to the smell "of childhood: a pleasant smell; flat and clean like paper" and then speaks of "the iron bonds of his imminent adulthood"

(*BI* 196). With his paper/iron analogy, the novelist clearly defines growth as an ambiguous dual process involving a positive movement from weakness to strength but also a negative movement from flexibility to rigidity. The *a contrario* moral that is given between the lines is that maturity only comes when accepting a series of inevitable renunciations and inflexible restrictions in life. Like Koch who seems to question the validity of swapping childhood for adulthood, readers are left to wonder whether a few smooth illusions are not worth an embittered reality.

The sad overtones of the esperectomic (i.e., hope-depriving) ending of *The Boys in the Island* is likely to affect readers, perhaps even more so the preadolescents and adolescents who got acquainted with Koch's debut novel through school curricula. As Roberta Trites puts it, "How we think about growth influences how we experience growth – and what we tell adolescents about their growth, in turn, has significant ramifications for their own conceptualisations of maturation" (8). Responding empathetically to Koch's nostalgia for the lost Edenic innocence of childhood, this younger readership may conceivably be made to deeply regret the transformation process and to adopt a more critical outlook on the less enchanting world of adults. In this respect, one can indeed make the safe claim that *Bildungsromane* enrich their readers cognitively.

Since the advent of research on brain plasticity in the 1970s, there has been no evidence disproving the fact that our brains are "culturally modified":

> Neuroplastic research has shown us that every sustained activity ever mapped – including physical activities, sensory activities, learning, thinking and imagining – changes the brain as well as the mind. Cultural ideas and activities are no exception. Our brains are modified by the cultural activities we do – be they reading, studying music, or learning new languages. We all have what might be called a culturally modified brain, and as cultures evolve, they continually lead to new changes in the brain.
>
> (Doidge 288)

Consequently, there is no denying that readers benefit from the aesthetic enrichment of reading novels, and more specifically *Bildungsromane*. There is also no denying that if you have remembered anything from your reading, your brain has changed. Nor is there any denying that the slightest thing you visualize in a novel (be it a location, a character, a voice, or a plot outcome) is an indication that your brain has changed and is therefore evidence of narrative impact. Yet, narrative *persuasion* – succinctly defined as the impact of narratives on readers as shown in their altered attitudes, beliefs, and behaviors – is a different kettle of fish and perhaps harder to substantiate with evidence. As Marco Caracciolo and Thom Van Duuren argue,

> Long-term changes can be demonstrated only through "longitu-dinal" studies, by monitoring the effects of reading over months or even years. However, this kind of experimental design is difficult to implement in practice, since disentangling the effects of reading from the effects of social interaction, TV watching, or any other activity borders on the impossible.
>
> (521)

What is more, no matter how willing we are to acknowledge that fiction books cause changes – albeit transient – in brain structures and functions, it is also fair to say that virtually no evidence has been produced to prove that consuming fiction stories has any long-term impact on human beings.[8] The very short timescale of most experiments in the field is an ongoing concern in the scientific com-munity, as illustrated by David Comer Kidd and Emanuele Castano specifying that their findings "show that reading literary fiction *tem-porarily* enhances [Theory of Mind]."[9] The same goes for neuroscientist Gregory Berns and his co-researchers who feel the need to qualify their results by adding: "It remains an open question for further study as to how lasting these effects are" (Berns, Blaine, Prietula, and Pye 599). Psychologists also admit the paucity of evidence by acknowledging that "little is known about long-term effects of persuasion through fiction" (Appel and Richter 115).

Admittedly, Koch has made many moral pronouncements and his work has a strong doctrinal theological undercurrent. Yet, the very fact that a great many critical discourses on narrative persuasion and valuable reading are tentative, conjectural, and nuanced demonstrates how speculative the literature-as-a-moral-laboratory thesis is.[10] So how could one sustain the claim that readers would gain moral enrichment from reading *The Boys in the Island* or any other Koch *Bildungsroman*-influenced fictional story? In the current state of research, we would be hard-pressed to claim that we have reliable and efficient ways of attesting to the moral development of the reader, or to scientifically prove that literature helps instill and grow a sense of ethics in readers which would morally enrich them. What Frank Hakemulder shrewdly observed in 2000 still holds nowadays, as current research on literary narrative impact has not yet proven that moral development could either be enhanced by reading activities, post-reading ones, or these two joined actions: "it remains to be seen whether empathic effects, moral development and the enhancement of critical thinking can be achieved by reading, or whether these effects are due to a combination of reading and post-reading tasks" (Hakemulder 49).[11]

Conclusion

The Boys in the Island, *Across the Sea Wall*, *The Doubleman*, and *Lost Voices* all borrow, in a more or less diffused fashion, some of the formal features that adequately characterize the literary tradition of formation through transformation. Koch's *Bildungsroman*-inspired novels typically contain this dual movement of gazing inward but also outward, by impacting readers. Indeed, if we redefine fiction as a rich cognitive linguistic artifact as cognitive literary studies would, and if we subscribe to the cognitive linguists' view that the use of culturally inflected language shapes or influences the way we conceptualize things, there is no doubt that Koch's character-oriented narratives can transform readers' ideas about psycho-emotional growth and maturation into adulthood. While moral enrichment is not guaranteed after reading the novels from cover to cover, it is likely that their aesthetics and cognitive value will affect the reader's brain.

For good measure, I should add that, day in and day out, we are all immersed in a dynamic state of flux that is constantly subject to changes, some of which are barely noticeable. So, change in itself – be it cognitive, psychological, emotional, ethical, or epistemological – is no feat and perhaps to be expected. Given that the conjectural nature of much of the current research in cognitive studies and neuroscience is not able to attest to the long-term effect of the persuasive force of literary narrative content, let alone to the significance of its impact on readers, discussions about literature's transformative potential are somewhat a sign of overoptimism. And there is nothing wrong with being prone to optimism, quite the opposite.

Notes

1 By unfortunately overlooking Morgenstern's "but also" conjunction, translator Tobias Boes wrongly argues that "the *Bildungsroman* gazes not inward, at the development of its fictional protagonist, but outward, into the real world and toward the development of its audience," when Karl Morgenstern specifically refers to a dual action (Boes 2009: 648).

2 "Books are either unleashed or occluded by the reader. We bring our life stories, our prejudices, our grudges, our expectations, and our limitations with us to books" (Hustvedt 137).

3 For a general discussion of the influence of narratives over readers, see part I (chapters 2–5) in T. Brock, J. Strange, and M. Green (eds.) *Narrative Impact: Social and Cognitive Foundations* (New York/Hove: Psychology P, 2002). As early as the mid-1980s, French literary theorist and philosopher Paul Ricœur has propounded his theory of narrative identity, which establishes a convincing association between literary reading and its impact on identity: see his *Temps et récit* (1983–1985) trilogy. Reading fiction has the ability to alter personality features, see M. Djikic et al., "On Being Moved by Art: How Reading Fiction Transforms the Self." *Creativity Research Journal* 21.1 (2009): 24–29. Two psychologists from the University of Cologne have concluded that exposure to fictional narratives does alter readers' beliefs over time: "fictional stories provide effective means for long-term shifts in people's real-world beliefs [...]" in M. Appel and T. Richter, "Persuasive Effects of Fictional Narratives Increase Over Time." *Media Psychology* 10 (2007): 128. Reading quality fiction increases theory of mind and empathy levels in readers. See T. Goldstein and E. Winner, "Enhancing Empathy and Theory of Mind." *Journal of Cognition and Development* 13.1 (2012): 19–37 and D. Comer Kidd and E. Castano, "Reading Literary Fiction Improves Theory of Mind." *Science* 342 (18 October 2013): 377–380. Having said this, as Suzanne Keen puts it, "there is no guarantee that an individual reader will respond empathetically to a particular representation." Suzanne Keen, "A Theory of Narrative Empathy." *Narrative* 14.3 (October 2006): 222. Gregory Berns and his colleagues observed "[l]ong-term changes in connectivity, which persisted several days after the reading," see G. Berns, K. Blaine, M. Prietula, and B. Pye, "Short- and Long-Term Effects of a Novel on Connectivity in the Brain." *Brain Connectivity* 3.6 (2013): 590. To see how the effects of literary reading might influence the moral development of readers, cf. F. Hakemulder, *The Moral Laboratory: Experiments Examining the Effects of Reading Literature on Social Perception and Moral Self-Concept* (Philadelphia, PA: John Benjamins Publishing, 2000).

4 "Much research has been directed at the processes by which change may occur. One idea is that the persuasive effect of entertaining narrative texts may lie partly in the degree of immersion of readers or film audiences in a story" (Sanford 243).

5 See also: "Like a promise or a marriage ceremony, texts of this genre produce the state of affairs they aspire to and invite readers to participate in the transformation" (Morgan 343).

6 Lakoff and Johnson further contend that

> New metaphors have the power to create a new reality. This can begin to happen when we start to comprehend our experience in terms of a metaphor, and it becomes a deeper reality when we begin to act in terms

> of it. If a new metaphor enters the conceptual system that we base our actions on, it will alter that conceptual system and the perceptions and actions that the system gives rise to.
>
> (145)

7   Scripts in cognitive narratology "are dynamic repertoires comprised of a series of sequences" (Trites 36). They aim at cognitive efficiency and can be seen as paradigmatic stories building our expectations into simplistic predictable patterns of how real-life events are meant to unfold (see Trites 36–39).

8

> The idea that the degree of immersion of readers in a narrative affects the degree of persuasion has been shown in a number of experiments. There is still, however, further research needed on how attitudes and behaviour can be changed on a long-term basis.
>
> (Sanford 264)

9   Italics mine. In that same article, the authors distinguish affective Theory of Mind as "the ability to detect and understand others' emotions" from cognitive Theory of Mind which they define as "the inference and representation of others' beliefs and intentions" (Kidd and Castano 377).

10 See the use of the MAY modal verb: "We distinguished literary from popular fiction and have focused on how reading fiction (in particular literary fiction) *may* change us, how it *may* enhance our thinking about ethical problems, and how it *may* sharpen awareness of norms and values" (Hakemulder 161, italics mine). Another example would be the use of the MIGHT modal verb: "[...] exposure to the literary arts, such as poetry and fictional literature, *might* provide a novel context for such thinking, and thus support the development of coherent life stories by helping to organise personal experience" (Mar, Peskin, and Fong 74, italics mine).

11 For a perceptive critique of Hakemulder's and Keith Oatley's experimental designs, see Caracciolo and Van Duuren (522–526).

Works Cited

Appel, Markus, and Tobias Richter. "Persuasive Effects of Fictional Narratives Increase Over Time." *Media Psychology* 10 (2007): 113–134.

Berns, Gregory, Kristina Blaine, Michael Prietula, and Brandon Pye. "Short- and Long-Term Effects of a Novel on Connectivity in the Brain." *Brain Connectivity* 3.6 (2013): 590–600.

Boes, Tobias. "Introduction to On the Nature of the *Bildungsroman*." *PMLA* 124.2 (2009): 647–649.

———. *Formative Fictions: Nationalism, Cosmopolitanism and the Bildungsroman*. Ithaca, NY: Cornell UP, 2012.

Brock, Timothy, Jeffrey Strange, and Melanie Green, eds. *Narrative Impact: Social and Cognitive Foundations*. New York/Hove: Psychology P, 2002.

Caracciolo, Marco, and Thom Van Duuren. "Changed by Literature? A Critical Review of Psychological Research on the Effects of Reading Fiction." *Interdisciplinary Literary Studies* 17.4 (2015): 517–539.

Cave, Terence. *Thinking with Literature: Towards a Cognitive Criticism.* Oxford: Oxford UP, 2016.

Djikic, Maya, Keith Oatley, Sara Zoeterman, and Jordan B. Peterson. "On Being Moved by Art: How Reading Fiction Transforms the Self." *Creativity Research Journal* 21.1 (2009): 24–29.

Doidge, Norman. *The Brain That Changes Itself.* Melbourne: Scribe, 2007.

Dolto, Françoise. *La Cause des adolescents.* Paris: Robert Laffont, 1988.

Goldstein, Thalia, and Ellen Winner. "Enhancing Empathy and Theory of Mind." *Journal of Cognition and Development* 13.1 (2012): 19–37.

Hakemulder, Frank. *The Moral Laboratory: Experiments Examining the Effects of Reading Literature on Social Perception and Moral Self-Concept.* Philadelphia, PA: John Benjamins Publishing, 2000.

Hulse, Michael. "C.J. Koch in Conversation with Michael Hulse in London." *Quadrant* 29.6 (1985): 17–25.

Hustvedt, Siri. *Living, Thinking, Looking.* London: Sceptre, 2012.

Keen, Suzanne. "A Theory of Narrative Empathy." *Narrative* 14.3 (2006): 207–236.

Kidd, David Comer, and Emanuele Castano. "Reading Literary Fiction Improves Theory of Mind." *Science* 342 (2013): 377–380.

Koch, Christopher. *Across the Sea Wall.* Sydney: Angus & Robertson, 1982.

———. *The Boys in the Island.* Sydney: Sirius, 1987.

———. *Crossing the Gap.* London: Chatto & Windus Ltd., 1987.

———. *The Doubleman.* Port Melbourne: Minerva, 1996.

———. *Lost Voices.* Sydney: Fourth Estate, 2012.

Lakoff, George, and Mark Johnson. *Metaphors We Live By.* Chicago/London: The U of Chicago P, 1980.

Mar, Raymond, Joan Peskin, and Katrina Fong. "Literary Arts and the Development of the Life Story." *New Directions for Child and Adolescent Development* 131 (2011): 73–84.

Morgan, Ben. "Embodied Cognition and the Project of the Bildungsroman: *Wilhelm Meister's Apprenticeship* and *Daniel Deronda.*" *Poetics Today* 38.2 (2017): 341–362.

Morgenstern, Karl. "On the Nature of the *Bildungsroman.*" *PMLA* 124.2 (2009): 650–659.

Oatley, Keith. *Such Stuff as Dreams: The Psychology of Fiction.* Malden, MA: Wiley-Blackwell, 2011.

Ricœur, Paul. *Temps et récit 1.* Paris: Le Seuil, 1983.

———. *Temps et récit 2: La configuration du temps dans le récit de fiction.* Paris: Le Seuil, 1984.

———. *Temps et récit 3: Le temps raconté.* Paris: Le Seuil, 1985.

Sanford, Anthony J. *Mind, Brain and Narrative.* Cambridge: Cambridge UP, 2012.

Sibony, Daniel. *Entre-deux. L'origine en partage*. Paris: Le Seuil, 1991.

Trites, Roberta Seelinger. *Literary Conceptualizations of Growth: Metaphors and Cognition in Adolescent Literature*. Philadelphia, PA: John Benjamins Publishing, 2014.

Žižek, Slajov. *The Parallax View*. Cambridge, MA: MIT P, 2006.

4 Australian High-Functioning ASD Fiction in the Age of Neurodiversity

Graeme Simsion's *Rosie* Trilogy

Introduction

The exploration of fiction dealing with high-functioning Autism Spectrum Disorder (ASD) – previously called Asperger's syndrome – is no novelty in Australian literature. The best-known earlier example is perhaps *The Secret Cure* (2003) by Sydney-based creative writer Sue Woolfe, who has also diligently fathomed the neuroscience of creative writing. Her novel came out in the same year as Mark Haddon's best-selling novel *The Curious Incident of the Dog in the Night-Time* (2003). Beyond the lavish chorus of praise and the international popular appeal, Graeme Simsion's *The Rosie Project* (2013) shares a few similar traits with Haddon's narrative: both are debut novels written by neurotypical writers dealing with high-functioning ASD; both protagonists (although from different generations) are scientific minds who do not see themselves as high-functioning autistic, no matter how markedly distinctive their psychopathological style is; and both of these first-person narratives are about an autistic savant embarking on a quest.

The Rosie Project and its sequels therefore fall within an emerging genre, that of high-functioning ASD fiction, which has come into prominence in the first decade of the twenty-first century.[1] Using the *Rosie* trilogy as a case study, I shall define the genre and list its most salient features before detailing how the neurodivergent mind style translates into a specific literary style. I will eventually discuss the politics of high-functioning ASD fiction and examine its heightened sense of advocacy.

Main Features and Definition of Australian High-Functioning ASD Fiction

High-functioning Autism Spectrum Disorder fiction is a subset of neurodivergence fiction, one of the five main literary subgenres[2]

DOI: 10.4324/9781003161455-6

featuring neurological narratives. The latter ultimately points to the self as an entangled sum of many constituent elements while occasionally exposing the felicities and limitations of brain science. In this section, I shall elaborate on the five major features with which high-functioning ASD fiction is identified, namely: a neurotypical narrative showing or espousing the mind style of a high-functioning ASD character; a narrator on the high-functioning spectrum stepping in the limelight; the difficulty for the neurodivergent character to achieve social inclusion; a brain-conscious narrative whose protagonist is essentially perceived as a cerebral organism; not to mention an ambiguous blend of autistic and scientific cultures.

Graeme Simsion is no aspie (i.e., a person who identifies as high-functioning autistic) sharing his insider's perspective of neurodivergence. This essentially means that his *Rosie* trilogy, like most ASD fictional narratives written by neurotypical authors who talk through a neurodivergent voice, is an exercise in literary ventriloquism. Although extraneous to their subject matter, these neurotypical writers "appropriate neurological difference in order to experiment with novel narration styles" (Tougaw 131) and create *sui generis* characters, rather than generic ones with which neurotypical readers would more readily identify. In a sense, it is fair to say that writers like Graeme Simsion are meddling with neurodiversity politics from the outside while bringing awareness to neurological difference in a more entertaining way than disabilities studies would. Yet, by doing so, Simsion faces possible charges of romanticizing the neurodevelopmental condition of individuals who are socially disenfranchised (Savarese and Zunshine 34–35).

In first-person high-functioning ASD fictional stories, the neurodivergent character takes center stage by taking up the role of a high-functioning ASD narrator. Although Professor Donald Tillman has previously been diagnosed with OCD[3] and has shown signs of having a haunting obsession with time, excessive planning and accuracy, he is more likely to have Asperger's syndrome in the light of all the evidence pooled in this chapter: mind-blindness resulting in social ineptitude, communication difficulties, emotional and behavioral issues, savantism,[4] diverse thinking, to name a few. Readers will even find out when perusing the final instalment of the trilogy, *The Rosie Result* (2019), that his atypical cognition was genetically passed on to his son, Hudson. Both father and son have "an aversion to changes in routine" (*The Rosie Result (RR)* 14) and possess superior ability in science. When some of the other characters try to bring up the subject of inherited autism, Don is rather nonconfrontational about the subject, and ASD is at best no more than a "hypothesis" in his mind (*RR* 35, 44, 81).

Not only do these neurodivergent characters single themselves out with their distinctive mind styles, but also with their struggle to adjust socially. Don sees himself as "socially inept" (*RP* 253)[5] and most of the misadventures on his bumpy journey arise just from "pragmatic failure" (Semino 142) and the fact that he has a logic and a modus operandi of his own, which is unfortunately not shared by the neurotypical community. For instance, Don is first mistaken for a pedophile and eventually for a terrorist in *The Rosie Effect* because of his atypical attitude. In addition, he is misunderstood to be a racist in *The Rosie Result*. What Don perceives as his social ineptitude has even become a major threat as his mind-blindness (or his inability to attribute mental states to others) could ruin his quaint Wife Project: "My concern was more with social faux pas. It would be terrible to lose the perfect relationship because I failed to detect sarcasm or looked into her eyes for greater or less than the conventional period of time" (*The Rosie Project (RP)* 152).

As if they were seen through a neuroscientist's eyes, these fictional stories are conspicuously informed by neuroscientific culture. On the one hand, they put a strong focus on the brain, mainly on its anatomy, its processes and its disorders.[6] On the other hand, they occasionally refer to scientific research, mainly studies in cognitive science and neuroscience (*RP* 130; *The Rosie Effect (RE)* 159, 188). When working at a cocktail bar for a group of doctors, Don blurts out his scientific knowledge: "'There is no experimental evidence of a correlation between synapse numbers and intelligence level within primate populations.' I recommend reading Williams and Herrup, *Annual Review of Neuroscience*" (*RP* 130). In this excerpt, Don mentions a genuine article co-written by Robert W. Williams and Karl Herrup that was published in 1988 under the title of "The Control of Neuron Number." Composed in the age of neural plasticity, the *Rosie* trilogy implicitly subscribes to the view that the brain is graced with the ability to adapt thanks to its amazing neuroplasticity. Neural plasticity therefore opens up the possibility of change through a "reconfigured mind."[7] In *The Rosie Effect*, Don is rising to a new challenge: he sets out to become a conventional father in New York. To this effect, he needs to improve himself by honing his socio-emotional skills to avoid his repeated pattern of getting into trouble over and over again.

Finally, there is a blurring of the boundaries between autistic and scientific cultures. The *Rosie* novels are undeniably peppered with scientific culture, as some parts of them are set in a scientific environment (i.e., the University Science Department). Furthermore, they involve a central character, 39-year-old Don Tillman, who is a high-functioning scientist. They also allude to, if not embrace, scientific research; not to mention the fact that they often make use of scientific terminology. Because Don is a genetics scholar by trade whose vocabulary is colored with marked technicality, it remains unclear whether his speech is meant to be a giveaway of his scientific mind or of his psychopathological style. For instance, his discussion of conceiving and raising a kid is couched in technical words in this sentence: "[...] I had actually done almost zero to prepare for baby production and maintenance, other than the purchase of ingredients for one pregnancy-compatible meal and the research excursion that led to the Playground Incident" (*RE* 154). When Don confesses "I was a scientist. I was autistic" (*RR* 374) in the last chapter of *The Rosie Result*, readers realize that Graeme Simsion has deliberately exploited this ambiguous overlap of autism and science throughout the *Rosie* trilogy.

With the latter and the subgenre's five salient traits in mind, Australian high-functioning ASD fiction can be defined as a brain-conscious fictional narrative which is most likely to be written by a neurotypical author. The plot tends to feature a major character who is depicted as having, or is identified by, a neurological condition formerly called Asperger's syndrome. While shedding new epistemological light on literary representations of interiority and subjectivity, these narratives of atypical cognition seem to normalize neurodivergence by blurring the lines between autistic and scientific cultures. These fictional experiments subtly fight ableism by paying tribute to the diversity of mind styles in an attempt to enrich ideas of selfhood and neurocosmopolitanism through counterfactual thinking and a tailored poetics of narrative.

From Mind Style to Literary Style: Narrating Neurodivergence

Like Johnathan Lethem, Mark Haddon, and Tom McCarthy, whose works Jason Tougaw discusses in his stimulating monograph entitled *The Elusive Brain: Literary Experiments in the Age of Neuroscience* (2018), Graeme Simsion writes "in a tradition of fiction narrated by or through characters with eccentric cognitive dispositions – many of them in direct dialogue with psychological theories, medical practice, or the philosophy of mind" (Tougaw 131). University Professor Donald Tillman is always embarking on personal projects and subprojects of all sorts. The very fact that he has projects of his own makes him quite unexceptional by world standards, but his odd relabeling of mundane activities into dead serious "projects" (The Wife Project, the Father Project, the Don Project, the Rosie Project, etc.) that are receiving his undivided attention turns him, by world standards again, into a peculiar protagonist with a specific mind style which translates into a peculiar literary style.

Like Christopher John Francis Boone in *The Curious Incident of the Dog in the Night-Time*, it seems that Professor Donald Tillman eschews clinical labels and medical diagnoses. Indeed, it is noteworthy that at no point does the author label his central character with ASD, nor do the protagonists see themselves as aspies. However, a few narrative pointers leave no doubt as to Professor Tillman being on the spectrum, as well as his ten-year-old son Hudson. In *The Rosie Result*, after overcoming his relationship crisis with Rosie, Don moves back to Melbourne and gets a new job. One of his colleagues, Professor Lawrence, has suspicions about Don's atypical behavior and asks him to entertain the possibility that he might be a "person with a disability" (*RR* 38):

> "I don't want you to take this the wrong way. But you're an unusual person. Perhaps not so unusual in the Science and Mathematics faculties. But, I was wondering, have you ever seen a psychologist?"
>
> "Why?"
>
> "I think even a layperson might guess that you were on the spectrum – the autism spectrum. I imagine I'm not the first person to suggest that."
>
> "Correct" […] "You're proposing that I claim to have Asperger's syndrome. Making me a member of a minority entitled to special consideration."
>
> "A person with a disability – and one relevant to the mistake you made. You'd need a formal diagnosis, if you don't already have one."
>
> (*RR* 38–39)

In parallel, the school principal asks Mrs. Rosie Jarman, a mental-health researcher, and Don Tillman, a professor of genetics, to have their son properly diagnosed (*RR* 41).

Don's clinical account of his adventure-packed daily existence – which at times reads like a scientific Powerpoint presentation with bullet points, options galore, exhaustive lists, guesstimates, calculations, recaps, informative facts and figures – is meant to convey his technical outlook on life. In this respect, the list on page 60 of *The Rosie Project* and the first three pages of chapter 35 of the same book, which inform neurotypical readers of the challenges of being neurodivergent, or chapter 2 of *The Rosie Result* in which Don makes a list of his current problems, are telling examples of that catalogue effect. Don's recasting everyday speech into technical terminology produces an alienating effect which puts him in a class of his own. Even his occasional quaint similes are imbued with the same technicality which colors the entire narrative: "Unlike the stereotypical wedding dress, it was – to use a mechanical term – *elegant*, like a computer algorithm that achieved an impressive outcome with just a few lines of code" (*RE* 186).

Don never misses an opportunity to acknowledge his neuro-divergence in *The Rosie Project*, although it is fair to say that this second-nature habit of his has been drastically downplayed in the 2014 and 2019 sequels. These narrative reminders tend to point to the existing gap between neurological difference and neurological norms. When not perceived through the neurodivergent character's eyes,[8] this marked difference is stylistically sugar-coated with a series of euphemisms and periphrases used by his fellow characters. His beloved Rosie, the eponymous Mrs. Jarman, sees him as "a strange man" (*RP* 116), "not exactly average" (*RP* 207), and expects "constant craziness" from her partner (*RP* 315). His best friend Gene tells him that his "old behaviour – was in a class of its own" (*RP* 283). Professor Lawrence, a colleague, characterizes Don as "an unusual person" (*RR* 38). The same applied to his son Hudson, who is seen by one of the school staff, Neil Warren, as "different" (*RR* 45).

To a certain degree, the *Rosie* trilogy shares common ground with disability studies and the more recent Mad Literary Studies (or Mad Humanities) by exuding antipsychiatry activism. The antipsychiatry movement construes psychiatry's branding of Asperger's syndrome as a "personality disorder" or as a "social deficit" (see Kapp, Gillepsie-Lynch, Sherman, and Hutman) to be an instrument of social control, which aims at stigmatizing individuals at odds with the neurotypical people who *statistically* stand for the norm. I emphasize the word "stat-istically" because, as Édouard Zarifian has it, "[t]here is no norm in itself, but only a consensus of the cultural group about what is normal behaviour and what is deviant" (Zarifian 46).[9] Antipsychiatry, as Joseph Berke reminds readers, perceives neurodivergence as "a social and cul-tural phenomenon" (Boyers and Orrill 209). In the opening pages of the first volume, the neurodivergent protagonist, who is about to lecture on high-functioning ASD, subscribes to this opinion:

> Naturally, the books and research papers described the symptoms of Asperger's syndrome, and I formed a provisional conclusion that most of these were simply variations in human brain function that had been inappropriately medicalised because they did not fit social norms – *constructed* social norms – that reflected the most common human configurations rather than the full range.
>
> (*RP* 6–7)

The Rosie Result is even more explicit in its rant against psychiatry (*RR* 192) with its tendency to overmedicate neurodivergent patient or systematically opt for "pharmaceutical solutions" (*RR* 107–108, 237).

To lighten the seriousness that disability-related topics command, the *Rosie* trilogy – sketchily defined as a cross between the David Lodge campus novel and the heart-warming romantic comedy – unsurprisingly adopts a comic tone. Donald Tillman has a zany rollercoaster story to tell, namely how, one day in Melbourne, he decided out of the blue that he would get married through an almost scientific protocol involving a thorough questionnaire. Graeme Simsion's screwball triptych comedy is taking high-functioning ASD fiction to an unprecedented humorous level that expunges all the gravity and pathos from his highly entertaining and yet sobering tale. Readers are therefore unlikely to experience compassion fatigue when binge-reading *The Rosie Project* (2013), *The Rosie Effect* (2014), and *The Rosie Result* (2019). Lightweight humor is used to alleviate the gravity of high-functioning ASD, such as when Don is caught in the middle of a controversy following his giving a seminar lecture which was largely misunderstood. As a result, "[t]he social-media exposure prompted three opinion pieces in the press, misrepresenting the facts and arguing that my behaviour was representative of a general malaise. This was new to me: I was accustomed to criticism for being unusual rather than typical" (*RR* 21).

Published in the wake of the Australian disability rights movement, which gained momentum in the 1980s, Graeme Simsion's narratives offer cultural representations that push back the well-entrenched stereotypes born of a neuronormative society, while indirectly agitating for social inclusion.

The Politics of High-Functioning ASD Fiction: "Aspies Rule!"

Graeme Simsion navigates a path through preconceptions of ASD – such as the blame for autism put on poor parenting (*RP* 13) or the use of two male high-functioning ASD characters that potentially implies that high-functioning ASD is a gender-marked trait[10] – and the set of media stereotypes that creative writers unwillingly contribute to when imagining autism. Indeed, unlike nonfiction writers who would espouse the clinical reality of ASD and its medical accuracies, it seems that the need for novelists to dramatize the ASD condition and make it recognizable to most readers can only be achieved by foregrounding the broadest of autistic features in the narrative. As Jason Tougaw points out, "Narrating neurodivergence risks dealing in caricatures of neurological difference, reinforcing stereotypes, or making readers feel they are gaining genuine knowledge from fictional portraits" (Tougaw 133).[11] However, in *The Rosie Result*, Simsion has found an astute way of countering preconceptions of ASD by highlighting these general representations in italics and juxtaposing them with the fictional reality he has constructed. Witness: "Hudson laughed briefly. *Autistic people often do not get jokes*" (*RR* 102).[12]

In *The Rosie Result*, Don is reluctant to broach the subject of autism when having a meeting with his son's Principal:

> "Do we now discuss the Asperger's hypothesis?" I asked.
> "Autism. Excuse me correcting you, but psychiatrists don't use the term Asperger's any longer and it's important that we stay up-to-date," said the principal. "What we used to call Asperger's we now understand as a milder form of autism. Which is what Neil is suggesting Hudson may have."
>
> (*RR* 44)

Mentioning autism in such an oblique way, by including passages touching on Asperger's syndrome without having any of the high-functioning ASD characters admitting to being on the spectrum is a strategic narrative ploy which has dual benefits. On the one hand, it enables creative writers who do not want to overstep their role to stay clear from becoming official advocates of the neurodiversity movement. On the other hand, it allows them to buffer the attacks they could receive from autism associations. The latter could either take exception to literary representations of disabilities because, as Jason Tougaw observes, these literary experiments often run the risk of being "received as portraits of lived neurological difference" (Tougaw 155), or autism associations could argue that neurotypical writers do not have the legitimacy to portray adequately neurodivergence, and more specifically autistic experience.

Thanks to the disability and neurodiversity movements that helped neurodivergent populations gain increased social prestige, the social vulnerability of people like Professor Donald Tillman promptly morphs into a "major advantage" that organizes itself around new paradigms (typical/atypical cognition, neurotypical/neurodivergent, etc.) and shapes up "the neurology of the self" (Alain Ehrenberg). When, at the outset of *The Rosie Project* (2013), Professor Donald Tillman gives a lecture on Asperger's syndrome in an inner-Melbourne suburban school, he is shocked to hear the convener say "It's nobody's fault" and corrects Julie without further ado: "Fault! Asperger's isn't a fault. It's a variant. It's potentially a major advantage. Asperger's syndrome is associated with organisation, focus, innovative thinking and rational detachment" (*RP* 11). This is an apt illustration of how high-functioning ASD narratives articulate the various situations in which neurological difference is valued, thus resonating with neurodiversity politics which seeks to protect the rights of neuro-atypical individuals. In doing so, Asperger's syndrome fiction contributes to raising the standing of neurodivergent populations while restoring them to favor.

In the light of the neurodiversity paradigm and of the rhetoric of disability, both of which encourage neurocosmopolitanism,[13] the social image of neuro-atypicality suddenly finds itself enhanced through empowerment. Resourceful Don comments perceptively on his condition:

> I accepted that I was wired differently from most people, or, more precisely, that my wiring was towards one end of a spectrum of different human configurations. My innate logical skills were significantly greater than my interpersonal skills. Without people like me, we would not have penicillin or computers.
>
> (*RE* 25)

In other words, what was previously seen as symptoms of a social handicap is now extolled as special gifts. Don comes across as "an innovative problem-solver" (*RR* 4) who possesses outstanding "innate logical skills," has the ability to predict people's body mass index and is extremely reliable when it comes to providing "scientific rigour" (*RE* 221). The implied message is that it might just require a change of viewpoint to realize that, far from coming across as disabled in a normocentric society, "Aspies rule!" (*RP* 12).

In *La mécanique des passions* (2018), French sociologist Alain Ehrenberg pinpoints a turn in the 1960s–1970s when ideals of self-fulfillment were extended to the sick, the disabled, the deviants, and the crippled, who were often locked away in what Erving Goffman called total institutions.[14] At the crossroads of biosocial and neurodiversity discourses, the concept of hidden potential has enabled these marginalized populations to realize themselves fully in the social sphere thanks to unexploited skills that only a fresh and unprejudiced neurotypical outlook could reveal. An apt illustration of this is found in the opening pages of *The Rosie Result* when Rosie manages to bring her partner's attention to one of his key skills of which he was unaware:

> It was satisfying that my partner recognised an attribute that I had not previously articulated. I was a good problem-solver. I had the

advantage of an atypical – the word used by others was *weird* – approach to analysing and responding to situations.

(*RR* 3–4)

By stressing the singularity and hidden potential of neurodivergent individuals, such as the ASD population that epitomizes an archipelago of differences, one is able to counter the medical discourse which sees these individuals as defective or as cognitive deficit patients who are judged against the stigmatizing canon of normocentrism.

Writers like Graeme Simsion de facto come across as public advocates for neurological difference, although bearing in mind the fact that "each autistic person is different in his or her own ways" (Hacking 636). Animated by a sense of social justice, their literary narratives are modelled on – but not generated by – neurodivergent mind styles and patterns of thinking. Their narrative content tends to be subversive by turning "the rhetorical tables on neurotypical norms – a common move in neurodiversity discourse" (Tougaw 105) and by pointing to the shortcomings of neurotypicality. For instance, at the end of *The Rosie Project* when Don declares his love to Rosie, Rosie hesitates in these terms:

"You're incredibly brave. I have the best fun with you, you're the smartest, funniest person I know, you've done all these things for me. It's everything I want and I've been too scared to grab it because –"

She stopped but I knew what she was thinking, I finished her sentence for her.

"Because I'm weird. Perfectly understandable. I'm familiar with the problem because everyone else seems weird to me."

Rosie laughed.

I tried to explain.

"Crying over fictitious characters, for example."

(*RP* 314–315)

In the passage above, Don manages to turn the situation around and to his advantage by claiming that neurotypical people also have weird behaviors. He goes on to illustrate his point with what is known as "the paradox of (emotional response to) fiction," namely the philosophical puzzle that argues that human beings respond irrationally to fiction, given that the fictional objects that move them do not exist.

When all is said and done, the *Rosie* trilogy is perhaps all about fostering a sense of caring[15] for the neurodivergent by helping readers empathize with Aspergic difference. In an early scene of *The Rosie Result*, Don and Rosie are attending an autism seminar. One of the participants, Liz, explains the concept of social disability by turning the tables: "Imagine everyone used wheelchairs, except you, and society was designed to accommodate them. You'd knock your head on door frames and have to ask for a chair at restaurants" (*RR* 65). This very technique, which enables fresh perspective-taking conducive to empathy, is put into practice midway in the novel with a reverse role-play of sorts. Don and Rosie finally open their bar designed to accommodate and attract a certain category of people: the non-neurotypical. At the end of *The Rosie Result*, the Tillmans are transferring their son to St. Benedict's, a special school. When headmaster Barry O'Connor meets the family and surveys their inclusive education policy and framework, a claim is being made for neurotypical people to show more empathy:

> Barry gave a short speech emphasising the school's acceptance of human diversity. It was similar to the speech we had been given by Bronwyn the Principal prior to enrolling Hudson, but Barry illustrated it with numerous examples, including some featuring autism.
>
> Whether or not Hudson met the diagnostic criteria for autism, it was encouraging to know that individual traits would be treated with understanding. I had observed that neurotypicals criticised autistic people for lacking empathy – towards *them* – but seldom made any effort to improve their own empathy towards autistic people.
>
> (*RR* 318)

Conclusion

By putting center stage a high-functioning ASD protagonist who has an acute awareness of being a brain-configured subject with atypical cognition, Graeme Simsion contributes to the increasing visibility of these cognitively different styles which shape up "a capability-based individualism."[16] Far from gloomily representing "autism [...] as a remorseless attacker of innocents, a destroyer of lives and families" (Murray 209), his *Rosie* trilogy frames high-functioning autism with a good-hearted and uplifting vision of neurodivergence, no matter how estranged this vision is from the clinical reality. These cultural representations could be instrumental in helping neurotypical readers come to a better understanding of, and even empathy with, cognitive difference, and contribute to a greater sense of social justice.

What these high-functioning ASD narratives essentially promote and exacerbate with a character whose brain is "being configured differently" (*RP* 205) is the neurological tenet that each individual is wired differently, and so, each individual is unique. Their irreducible singularity is mostly epitomized by their *sui generis* mind style and original lifestyle. Perhaps the idea of a hidden, if not outstanding, potential which needs to be revealed and duly exploited lies at the heart of every single one of us, who are worthy just the way we are.

Notes

1 See Ian Hacking's article for a comprehensive survey of autism fiction published in 2000–2010.
2 The other four being: brain nonfiction (brain memoirs, brain science books, brain-focused creative nonfiction, etc.), neurodivergence nonfiction (memoirs, autobiographies, etc., essentially written by neurodivergent authors), neuronovels (with brain-centered plots), and neuro-graphic novels.
3

> Somewhere in a medical archive is a twenty-year-old file with my name and the words "depression, bipolar disorder? OCD?" And schizophrenia? The marks are important – beyond the obvious observation that I was depressed, no definitive diagnosis was ever made, despite attempts by the psychiatric profession to fit me into a simplistic category.
>
> (*RP* 205)

What is more, Don is euphemistically described in *The Rosie Effect* as "a highly organised person who avoid[s] uncertainty and like[s] to plan in detail" (*RE* 389). It should be noted that Grace Lisa Vandenberg in Toni Jordan's *Addition* (2008) and Howard Hughes in Luke Davies' *God of Speed* (2008) are proto-examples of characters whose obsessive compulsive disorder (OCD) has set a precedent in the portrayal of cognitive disability in Australian fiction.
4 In discussing the proliferation of autism stereotypes, Douwe Draaisma notes that "the majority of cases of autism do not have savantism" (1477) and further adds that "It is often mentioned that the stereotype of the autistic savant raises expectations to an unrealistic level, causing disappointment and frustration for the many autistic persons not so gifted" (1478).
5 Don's lack of social skills is a leitmotiv in the opening chapter of *The Rosie Project*: "I have never found it easy to make friends" (*RP* 3); "Restaurants are minefields for the socially inept, and I was nervous as always in these situations" (*RP* 4); "Afterwards, Claudia advised me that I should have abandoned the experiment prior to Elizabeth leaving. Obviously. But at what point? Where was the signal? These are the subtleties I fail to see" (*RP* 6). Similar self-deprecating comments are to be found in the sequels: "I'm somewhat socially incompetent" (*RE* 104), etc.

6 For mentions of the brain anatomy, see *RP*: "cerebellum" 60, "synapses" 129, "brain stem" 252. For the references to brain processes, see *RP*: "cognitive load" 60, "brain overload" 151, "cognitive functions" 163, "brain malfunction" 207, "emotional overload" 252, "My brain was already overloaded" 301; *RE* "There was an extraordinary amount to process, and my brain was now functioning normally, or at least in the manner I was accustomed to" 27, "There are vast numbers of things I don't tell you. You'd have information overload" 115, "More material to process" 152, "to protect Rosie from distress and both Bud and her from the harmful effects of excess cortisol" 200, "Impairment of cognitive function is a common side-effect of pregnancy" 268, "I had vast amounts of confusing information to process" 360 and *RR*: "My brain was in danger of becoming overloaded" 30, "I have a particular brain configuration" 40, "I guessed he was losing some cognitive function" 135, "My brain was wired for honesty" 363. Graeme Simsion has shown a growing concern for mental health issues over the course of the three instalments. For allusions to cognitive disorders, see *RP*: "the benefits to my mental health justify the risks" 124, "Somewhere in a medical archive is a twenty-year-old file with my name and the words 'depression, bipolar disorder? OCD?' And schizophrenia?" 205; *RE*: "early-onset Alzheimer's or some other form of dementia" 118, "clinically depressed" 125, "postnatal depression risk" 138, "postpartum psychosis" 304; and *RR*: "bipolar disorder" 13, "clinically manic" 99, "ADHD, OCD, anxiety disorder, bipolar disorder, early onset schizophrenia, personality disorder" 254, to name a few.

7 For references attesting to the reversibility of autistic features, to Don's behavioral change and to the brain's capacity for self-reconfiguration, see *RP*: 197, 232, 284, 289; *RE*: 12, 179, 265, 320, 393, 408–409. *RR*: 11, 139, 328, 367–368.

8 Don's insistence on being different frequently transpires in his discourse: "people with uncommon attributes" (*RP* 14), "I have some unusual characteristics" (*RP* 179), "Unlike many people, I am very comfortable with repetition" (*RP* 193), "I think it is likely that my brain is wired in a non-standard configuration" (*RP* 248), "Unlike Gene and Claudia, and apparently the majority of the human race, I am not emotionally affected by love stories. I don't appear to be wired for that response" (*RP* 256), "I had eliminated a number of unconventional mannerisms from my vocabulary" (*RP* 283), "I was wired differently" (*RP* 310), "Because I'm weird" (*RP* 314), "[...] considering that I am supposedly wired differently" (*RP* 320).

9 My translation of: "Il n'existe pas de norme en soi, mais seulement un consensus du groupe culturel sur ce qui est comportement normal et ce qui est comportement déviant."

10 Stuart Murray explains the recurrence of the male figure in these terms:

> In accounts of Asperger's, whether in fiction or memoir, the stress on the male figure is even more pronounced. The kind of interests and obsessions – science, mathematics, calendars and timetables – associated with a figure like Daniel Tammet seem to be paradigmatically male

concerns, almost extensions of an idea of male personalities. Autism, it appears, can be understood best when seen in terms of the male character, and while its presence within females cannot be denied, it seems more difficult to map an idea of the condition on to the generalized sense of what we believe girls and women to be. Given that two of the most high-profile figures with autism – Temple Grandin and Donna Williams – are women, this appears especially counterintuitive.

(Murray 140)

11 Tougaw further explains in the next paragraph:

Of course, the cultural effects of any novel are variable and unpredictable, but they are shaped in part by the dynamics in reading established by the writer's formal choices. These particular novels require readers to immerse themselves in their narrator's mind styles, and they create powerful protagonists whose "creative potential" is directly linked with their neurological differences. They may provoke readers to reconsider their relations to cognitive norms, or they may provide a comfortable outlet reaffirming those norms.

(Tougaw 133)

12 This same technique has been used over and over again in *The Rosie Result*: 114, 140, 191, 227, 299.

13 Neurocosmopolitanism is defined by Savarese and Zunshine as "the idea of a trans-neurocommunity, the feeling of being respectfully at home with all manner of neurologies" which entails "a denaturalization, even a dethronement, of privileged neurotypicality" (Savarese and Zunshine 20).

14

Nous passerons ensuite de l'individualisation du patient au nouvel individualisme émergeant au cours des années 1960–70: les idéaux d'accomplissement personnel s'étendent à de nouvelles populations – malades, handicapés, déviantes, infirmes –, des populations vivant une expérience de la négativité dont le destin était bien souvent l'enfermement dans une institution. L'accomplissement consiste à retourner la négativité en la transformant en style de vie ayant une valeur, acceptée socialement: s'accomplir non seulement quels que soient les maux dont chacun est atteint, mais peut-être plus encore *grâce* à eux en découvrant son propre potentiel caché est devenu un des plus puissants idéaux de la condition autonome.

(Ehrenberg 27)

15 In Stuart Murray's sense of the word, that is "caring understood as a process of acknowledging, of thinking about, of admitting, debating, listening and sharing" (Murray 212).

16 My translation of "un individualisme de capacité" (Ehrenberg 50).

Works Cited

Boyers, Robert, and Robert Orrill, eds. *Laing and Anti-Psychiatry*. Harmondsworth: Penguin, 1972.

Draaisma, Douwe. "Stereotypes of Autism." *Philosophical Transactions of the Royal Society B: Biological Sciences* 364.1522 (27 May 2009): 1475–1480.

Ehrenberg, Alain. *La mécanique des passions: cerveau, comportement, société.* Paris: Odile Jacob, 2018.

Hacking, Ian. "Autism Fiction: A Mirror of an Internet Decade?" *University of Toronto Quarterly* 79.2 (2010): 632–655.

Kapp, Steven, Kristen Gillepsie-Lynch, Lauren E. Sherman, and Ted Hutman. "Deficit, Difference, or Both? Autism and Neurodiversity." *Developmental Psychology* 49.1 (2013): 59–71.

Murray, Stuart. *Representing Autism: Culture, Narrative, Fascination.* Liverpool: Liverpool UP, 2008.

Savarese, Ralph James, and Lisa Zunshine. "The Critic as Neurocosmopolite; Or, What Cognitive Approaches to Literature Can Learn from Disability Studies: Lisa Sunshine in Conversation with Ralph James Savarese." *Narrative* 22.1 (2014): 17–44.

Semino, Elena. "Pragmatic Failure, Mind Style and Characterisation in Fiction about Autism." *Language and Literature* 23.2 (2014): 141–158.

Simsion, Graeme. *The Rosie Project.* Melbourne: Text Publishing, 2013.

———. *The Rosie Effect.* Melbourne: Text Publishing, 2014.

———. *The Rosie Result.* Melbourne: Text Publishing, 2019.

Tougaw, Jason. *The Elusive Brain: Literary Experiments in the Age of Neuroscience.* New Haven/London: Yale UP, 2018.

Zarifian, Édouard. *Les Jardiniers de la folie.* Paris: Odile Jacob, 1988.

Part III

Cognition and the Body

Both cognitively informed essays in this new section seek in their own ways to discuss positive and negative representations of the body in non-Indigenous and Indigenous Australian literature. The first one defines the roles erotica and sexual arousability play in the reader's endogenous attention. Moving away from sexually explicit narratives to human disenfranchisement, the second discussion offers a comparative study of two Western Australia Indigenous narratives dealing with post-1788 Aboriginal history and colonization-related cultural trauma. The chapter shows how Claire Coleman and Doris Pilkington have utilized denotative language to expose the psychic pain through *externalized* signs of malaise, vulnerability, and dejection.

DOI: 10.4324/9781003161455-7

5   The Erotics of Writing and Reading Australian Fiction

Linda Jaivin, Frank Moorhouse, and John Purcell's Art of Dealing with Dirt

Introduction

Seeking to challenge the conservative and heteronormative views preva-lent in Australian society right up until the 1970s, a group of daring fiction writers specialized in the art of dealing with dirt, a word under-stood here as licentious subject matter. Thanks to the post-Chatterley liberalization of sexual expression in fiction, Australian literary pornog-raphy eventually developed and expanded while some more mainstream writers concerned with realism, such as Frank Moorhouse and Michael Wilding, included explicit graphic scenes and discussions of sexual relationships in their novels. Although the exploitation of sex in literary texts became the hallmark of a knot of writers like Venero Armano and Peta Spear, it also featured as a key ingredient in subgenres like grunge and erotica fiction.

In this chapter, I foreground the evolution of the sexual revolution in print by surveying three key periods in Australian literary history: the Balmain Group counterculture in the 1970s, the flourishing of grunge fiction in the 1990s, and the more contemporary twenty-first-century experiments with erotic fiction. I then discuss how Frank Moorhouse's, Linda Jaivin's, and John Purcell's poetics of sex differ before analyzing the cognitive implications of the use of erotic titilation and graphic sex scenes in literature.

The Sexual Revolution in Print: From the Balmain Group Era to Contemporary Erotica

In the wake of the 1960 *Lady Chatterley's Lover* obscenity trial, which led to the liberalization of sexual expression in fiction, combined with the American Sexual Revolution and its associated counterculture, which gained momentum at the same time, the relaxation of Australian

DOI: 10.4324/9781003161455-8

censorship in the 1970s allowed fiction writers to be more daring in their depictions or discussions of sexualities. Meanwhile, in other parts of the world, the publishing industry was jumping on the bandwagon of sexual liberation politics by releasing sex manuals of all kinds. It is this peculiar context of multiple converging factors which made it possible for a wind of libertine and libertarian change to sweep over the Australian literary panorama and open up new perspectives.

At the end of the 1960s, Frank Moorhouse along with a few other writers loosely constituted the "Balmain Group," whose name takes after what was at the time the grungy leavings of a working-class industrial hub, west of central Sydney. What is now known as the Balmain Group of Writers is a loose aggregate of emerging Australian writers who occasionally saw one another at bohemian parties but never congregated specifically for discussions on creative writing. Although the Balmain Group of Writers has drafted no manifesto to set sexual aesthetics and politics on the literary agenda, it seems that a certain freedom of expression in relation to the literary treatment of sex characterizes the fictitious stories from that era.

The counterculture revolution of the 1960s–1970s, encouraged by unashamed hedonism, was an anti-establishment movement which liberated sexual expression equally in homes and in print. This sociocultural context was conducive to newly recognized forms of sexual politics that challenged the heteronormative mindset of the times while opening up new vistas for apprehending the diverse range of invisiblized sexual behaviors. The loosening of censorship combined with the emancipatory social movements of the early 1970s had crystallized around the inclusion of representations of sexualities into narratives by the Balmain Group fiction writers bent on showing alternative domestic lifestyles. It is most fitting that Frank Moorhouse, whose stories were the target of censorship as early as in the 1950s and who was a spearheading figure in the anti-censorship campaigns of the 1970s, should come to symbolize this sexual revolution in print. For him, discussing sex transgressively might have had the same liberating and empowering effect as the actual experience of having sex. Such freedom of sexual expressiveness certainly broadened the Australian erotic fiction repertoire, or at least, it paved the way for more daring representations of bodily activity in Australian fiction, especially when the mention of sex was more tentative: i.e., simply discussed among characters or by the narrator rather than having their physical exploits depicted more directly. Moorhouse was therefore instrumental in developing the poetics and politics of sexuality that later authors like Linda Jaivin and John Purcell would take up and expand in their spicy writings by showing their characters' colorful sex lives.

Like Helen Garner's *Monkey Grip* (1977) and Andrew McGahan's *Praise* (1992), Linda Jaivin's *Eat Me* (1995) is, with hindsight, a canonical text of Australian grunge fiction (see Vernay "Sex in the City"). Broadly speaking, this literary subgenre mainly deals with dissatisfied sub/urbanites who endeavor to fill the vacuity and spleen of their existence with music, drugs, sexual delight, and intoxication. Obviously enough, most – if not all – definitions of grunge fiction portray sex as an attractive cop-out for these Australian characters. Grunge fiction writers like Linda Jaivin achieve a sense of intimacy thanks to the confessional mode of their narrators and to the autobiographical lineaments of their narratives, a typical trait of debut novels.

Unlike Helen Garner's debut novel, which can neither be labelled erotic nor pornographic, Linda Jaivin's *Eat Me*, which the author understates as "comic erotica" (Jaivin 30), reads like the archetypal plotline of a blue movie: namely, a string of fantasies climaxing into an orgiastic sexual frenzy. Needless to say that *Eat Me* is unashamedly democratic in its spanning of a variety of sexual activities, ranging from the erotica to the exotica: the opening chapter involves deviationist practices like stuffing, sadomasochism, and exhibitionism while the following chapters contain additional sexual experimentations such as allusions to voyeurism, transvestism, not to mention felching – i.e., the practice of introducing animals into the vagina or anus – in the penultimate chapter. As a quasi anagram of "tease me," Jaivin's fiction deals with the tantalizing fantasies of four femmes fatale: Chantal, Julia, Philippa, and Helen. In some respects, Jaivin and Philippa's blow-by-blow account of women's fantasies reminds us that our consumer society tends to overemphasize sexual feats no matter how they are achieved.

When all is said and done, sex in grunge narratives appears to be an unromantic physical enterprise motivated by instant self-gratification. Female sexuality in *Eat Me* finds as much its fulfillment in imaginary constructs as in fictional reality with domination-based scenarios, whether the female characters appear empowered or disempowered. Xavier Pons' remark in his discussion of erotic writing in Australia is most relevant to grunge fiction. This French scholar argues that sex can be seen as "sometimes a symptom, and sometimes an illustration, of the discontent which pervades civilisation" because "the dispirited characters have a lot of dispirited sex" ("Erotic Writing In Australia – Then and Now" 276).

In literary pornography, sex scenes are often the fruit of fantasy-packed scenarios that involve round-the-clock available over-bosomed nymphomaniacs and priapism-struck oversexed men, which is close to what readers are confronted with in *Eat Me*. John Purcell's *The Girl on the Page* (2018) flirts with this risqué commercial genre while simultaneously being an attempt to raise the literary standards of this popular "mummy porn" category, which focuses on the sexual fantasies and experiences of a central female character. His most recent novel, to date, was published 15 years after the anonymous release of Nikki Gemmell's erotica milestone in 2003. Like *The Girl on the Page*, the plot-line of *The Bride Stripped Bare* is no alibi for cramming it with sex scenes galore. Rather, it tells the juicy story of a woman's sexual journey who surrenders to her innermost desires. As for John Purcell, he wrote his way to erotic fame under the female nom de plume of Natasha Walker with his trilogy entitled *The Secret Lives of Emma* (2012), published hot on the heels of E.L. James' *Fifty Shades of Grey* (2011), whose best-selling trilogy paved the way for Purcell's success. At that same time, other Australian erotica writers were emerging like Kate Belle, who had three raunchy love stories published in 2013: *The Yearning*, *Breaking the Rules*, and *Bloom*.

The pornification of Australian fiction, whose wantonness is also attracting a wider array of readers, mainly thrives on the commercial dictum that "sex sells" (*Eat Me* (*EM*) 10), thus highlighting the interaction the publishing industry has with sex. Unsurprisingly, both *Eat Me* and *The Girl on the Page* metatextually reflect this close association. In Jaivin's fiction, Chantal is a fashion editor and Philippa an erotic writer-cum-journalist working on a lubricious novel which, according to her feminist friend Helen, should be called "Eat Me" (*EM* 15). In John Purcell's fiction, most sex scenes involve the casual sexual relationship Amy Winston has with her impromptu lovers (such as the unattractive Daniel Taylor, or Ehsan, the Iranian who stands for any Tom, Dick, or Harry with whom Amy has sex). Some of these impromptu lovers end up being regulars, like aspiring writer Josh and pot-boiler author Liam Smith, two well-hung alpha males Amy enjoys having rough sex with.

Like *Eat Me*, *The Girl on the Page* is "caught in that no man's land between commercial fiction and literature" (*Girl on the Page* (*GP*) 184). Like *Eat Me* again, *The Girl on the Page* goes into salacious detail from the very first pages, which sets the tone for the racy nature of the book's content: a promise for more sexual dalliance down the track. Book editor Amy is caught *in medias res* with a random stranger whose disrobed state leaves no suspense as to what has previously occurred and/or as to what might happen next: "He was standing there completely naked – tats, six-pack, stubble, enormous package – definitely bar staff" (*GP* 1). With John Purcell, the sexual revolution in print has therefore taken a new turn by upgrading commercial erotic fiction with a slightly literary edge. Indeed, the driving focus of this England-based story remains Amy Winston's efforts to retrieve some manuscript from acclaimed writer Helen Owen, who must justify with her productive creativity the substantial advance she has received from her publisher.

While Frank Moorhouse, Linda Jaivin, and John Purcell all master to some degree the art of dealing with dirt, their licentious subject matter seems to take different forms in their steamy writings.

The Erotics of Writing Sex in Text

The subversive Australian counterculture of the 1970s questioned and directly challenged mainstream heteronormativity by highlighting a generation gap between an older generation clinging onto traditional pre-feminist ideas of sexualities attached to family values and a more liberated group of people – some of whom referred to as hippies – who discussed sexual orientation more freely and who were keen to explore the joyous repertoire of sex, as portrayed in Moorhouse's *The Americans, Baby*. By creating a sexually provocative set of texts that would demarginalize and legitimize forms of sexualities that were given more visibility in Australian culture following the sexual revolution, Frank Moorhouse was blurring the lines of clear-cut sexual distinctions and practices. In doing so, he was diligent in depicting relationships and sociological communities that were not sufficiently widespread to be integrated into the norm: homosexuals, whether closeted like Carl or openly gay like Paul (see "The American Paul Jonson," "Who is Sylvia," "Jonson's Letter"), bisexuals (see "The Letters to Twiggy") and cross-dressers (see "Becker and the Boys from the Band"). Beyond the sexual freedom of unattached individuals who were encouraged to be sexually adventurous by engaging with a bountiful array of sexual practices (barring the illegal deviant ones such as pedophilia or zoophilia – both of which are alluded to in *The Americans, Baby*), there was the breaking of an even greater taboo: open relationships! These affairs directly challenged monogamous couples whose sexuality was held within the confines of autoerotism and one-to-one fornicative sessions.

In *The Americans, Baby: A Discontinuous Narrative of Stories and Fragments* (1972), which displays the occasional inclusion of some crude anatomical descriptions, sexual intercourse is depicted as part and parcel of a naturalistic tableau. These sexualized narratives, which can neither be labelled erotic nor pornographic, offer a greater sense of verisimilitude, the bedrock of realism which has always been prevalent in Australian novels. Therefore, it can be argued that *The Americans,*

Baby stretched the boundaries of the Australian novel genre by being inclusive of the intimacy of characters which up until the 1970s was prudishly censored. Frank Moorhouse shows no restraint in discussing sex and does not hesitate to call a spade a spade or – more to the point – a prick a prick. The author comes across as quite daring and democratic in his exploration of a wide gamut of sexual practices in *The Americans, Baby*: straight anal sex, group sex, same-sex intercourse, hand job, casual sex, extra-marital affairs, intergenerational sex, autoeroticism, (mutual) oral sex, and sexual fantasies.

Moorhouse's insightful observations of interpersonal rapport and seduction take the sexual element to be the cornerstone of human nature and desire. His "discontinuous narrative" technique,[1] which gives episodic insights into the lives of his characters, make heterosexual or homosexual sexual intercourse appear like a long conversation which could be interrupted, resumed, or terminated at any time. Amusingly, *Conference-Ville* (1976) uses, within the span of a chapter, the idea of a continuum of sexual sociability which bonds characters over time:

> I think we were both drawing on leftover intimacy of the affair we'd had a couple of years earlier. [...] We were pleased to find in bed that there was some of the intimacy left, and we were able to relax each other. The sex itself, though, was more caressing than passionate. In the after-sex rambling and cantor, we talked about earlier times.
>
> (*Conference-Ville* (*CV*) 56)

In Moorhouse's politically inflected "stories and fragments," sexual encounters are seldom allusively portrayed. On the contrary, they feature in more straightforward accounts, no matter how scandalous the 1970s readership might have deemed them to be.

However, the author would occasionally use an oblique way to include more hardcore material like deviant practices. There is no first-degree representation of characters practicing zoophilia, but there is a second-degree depiction of it. It is subtly reported as a story run by a fictitious newspaper, namely one pertaining to the counterfactual world Moorhouse imagined in "Soft Drink and the Distribution of Soft Drink": "Becker had once, and only once, read an obscene New York newspaper called the *National Expose*. There was something from that paper which described a girl and a dog" (*The Americans, Baby* (*AB*) 169). Similarly, in the climaxing story titled "The Letters to Twiggy," a 36-year-old Senior Lecturer in History has pedophilic sexual fanta-sies about raping teenage British model Twiggy, disturbing fantasies which he expresses in an anonymous letter (*AB* 218–219). Were they

not part of an aesthetic project, these two pages of crude depictions in
The Americans, Baby could be construed as pedopornographic material:

> I'm coming across to England and will drag you off to a motel and
> rip your beautiful Protor and Babbs Carnaby Street clothes off and
> your little silk panties, tie your hands and legs to the bed and ram
> my prick up your little girl's twat until you scream with pain.
>
> (AB 218)

The graphic fantasies even take a bisexual turn in which Twiggy, abu-
sively addressed in this letter as "Twatty," is imagined to be a sex-starved
gay twink. Twiggy, Twatty, twink: Moorhouse slips from one idea to the
next through lexical kinships and phonetic associations (the /tw/ allit-
eration in this instance). Twiggy's name being evocative of "twat" gives
rise to a sex-inflected story while the further phonetic association with
"twink" gives it a bisexual twist.

Unlike the socially interactive sex to be found in the narratives by
the Balmain Group of writers, depictions of sexual practices and desire
in grunge fiction are largely predatory and *Eat Me* is no exception in
this matter. In Jaivin's heterocentric narrative, the polyandrous sexual
behavior of Philippa Berry, Helen/Ellen, Julia/Jody, and Chantal/
Camilla responds to a basic drive and need in these women that expose
their desire as pertaining to the animal type, as opposed to the amorous
monogamous type (see Pasini, *La Force du désir* 75). Sex is appetizing
and sexual predation leads to devouring, as praying mantises would.
Eat Me, which can be read as a letter-dropping version of "Eat Men,"
clearly draws on the myth of "vagina dentata" defined in the novel
as "the classic unreconstructed male anti-fantasy: the fear of being
castrated by a cunt" (*EM* 174). If pornography is construed as the eroti-
cization of power, then clearly the power rests in the hands of these
strong-minded intellectual women who, either in reality or in fantasy,
prey on men and sexually objectify them. The androphagous predation in this novel corroborates Freud's intuition, in *Three Essays on the
Theory of Sexuality* (1905), that food and sex are interrelated, an association which Italian psychiatrist Willy Pasini took up and elaborated on
in his 1994 book, *Il cibo e l'amore*.

Verging on erotica fiction, Jaivin's narrative unsurprisingly
overemphasizes the penis with their warts-and-all depictions of women
serviced by rock-hard and oversized erections. Jaivin's characters go
through out-of-the-ordinary sexual experiences precisely because the
most unlikely the situation, the greater the arousal for readers. However,
the fact that some of Jaivin's characters feed on sexual fantasies might

betray sexual frustration or a kind of inadequacy which – incidentally – is not a gender-marked trait in grunge fiction. The representation of sex in fiction is subject to the overshadowing importance of the phallus – symbolizing desire and want – which is repeatedly mistaken for the penis. While the consequences of the disharmony between the representation of desire and its expression diverge according to the gender orientation of scenarios, symbols will be systematically tacked onto physiological realities. Through the eyes of female writers, man's *membrum virilis* will almost be systematically overrepresented, indicating not so much man's overriding desire for his partner as how strongly women feel to be desired:

> Would you believe, and I'm not exaggerating, his dick was so big that, in fact, I actually couldn't roll on the condom – he had to show me how to stretch it out with my fingers and pull it on that way.
>
> (*EM* 51)

If literary pornography were chiefly defined as a genre whose primary effect is to trigger sexual arousal, it is doubtful whether John Purcell's inclusion of passages sketching sexual intercourse in often less than ten lines would qualify as such, no matter how randy his characters are. The sex scenarios in *The Girl on the Page* appear to be quite tame in comparison with the blatantly norm-breaking ones to be found in *The Americans, Baby* and *Eat Me*, which are telling examples of "transgressive pornography," as Michael Newall conceives it.[2] Yet, the soft porn couplings in Purcell's novel – despite their being exclusively heterosexual and too mundanely conventional to be seen as dissident sexual practices – are still transgressive in their libertarian choices, as exemplified by the occasional depictions of "sex between strangers" and "sex in public places."

The largely heterosexual woman-centered erotica in *Eat Me* and *The Girl on the Page* is bound to address a female readership in priority as "research has shown that women have a better response to woman-centred erotica" (Doornwaard et al. 359). However, it is fair to highlight that Linda Jaivin is more adept than John Purcell at building sexual tension for which she prepares the ground over a few pages, thus creating an intellectual foreplay of sorts which channels her readers' selective attention. By contrast, Purcell's erotica scenes are more diegetically contained,[3] less signposted (thus giving the impression of random sex) and almost systematically focused on penile performance (size, vigor, and sexual satisfaction) with a heavy insistence on penis-oriented intercourse (*GP* 22–23, 51–52, 129, 151, 161, 198–201, 210–211). The fact that the *membrum virilis* is invariably referred to as "cock" – an influence from male pornography – and that the woman's genitals are hardly ever mentioned, save once and in a euphemistic way at that ("Liam stood, ran the tip of his cock against my wet lips, then grabbed my hips," *GP* 199) is a giveaway of the gender-specific nature of this male viewpoint on sexuality. This observation comes all the more as a surprise as Amy Winston is the female narrator and focalizer of the story.

Beyond its obvious aesthetic appeal as a novel literary concern, the pending question resulting from the sexualization of fictitious narratives is to determine whether or not sex in text is more than a mere commercial trick designed to boost book sales.

The Subtle Art of Dealing with Dirt: The Erotics of Reading Sexually Explicit Fiction

Through the subtle scenography and careful curation of its literary representations, the novel as a genre has a capacity for offering a mediation of reality, which is most convenient when the subject matter – like having open relationships, fantasizing over deviant sexual practices, or having casual sex with strangers – would be deemed too offensive or displeasing in real life. While this mediation of reality is generally dismissed as "entirely fictitious," literary representations of sexuality are, to a large extent, still toned down through euphemistic and suggestive depictions, lest the salacious texts be branded as indecent or pornographic and fall under censorship laws.

While representations of sexual desire can be repressed, desire per se cannot. Indeed, one of the major psychodynamics inherent to literature is that it responds to the desires of readers. These desires are epitomized as much by their horizons of expectations as by their craving need to interpret fiction and share their emotional responses to literary aesthetics. In this game of literary seduction, the writer's and the reader's desires are conflated through shared interests which, in the present case of erotica fiction, are sexuality and intimacy.

Admittedly, Freud's various intuitions have largely contributed to turning the harmony between creativity and sexuality into a truism. First, Freud's theory of the libido makes sexual energy the bedrock of all human activity, as discussed in *Three Essays on the Theory of Sexuality* (1905). Second, Freud advances the concept of sublimation, a process that realizes the mutation of the sexual drive (*Trieb*) into professions, especially artistic ones, "apparently unrelated to sex, but finding their aptitude in the force of sexual instinct" (Laplanche and Pontalis 465). Stylistically speaking, the inclusion of sex and the courageous depictions of alternative lifestyles and sexualities in the corpus under scrutiny (namely gang banging, gay sex, or random sex in *The Americans, Baby*; fisting, group sex, or felching in *Eat Me*; and sex between strangers or public sex in *The Girl on the Page*) are as much a manifestation of the author's sublimated sexual drive (which morphs into literary representations of sexual desire) as they are the essence of the characters' sexual energy in the fictitious worlds of Moorhouse, Jaivin, and Purcell. Therefore, these sexualized stories have intriguingly become the vehicle for venting the sexual drive of which literature is meant to be the sublimation.

It could also be argued that sex in text is utilized as a seductive lever to bring a wider audience to take a vested interest in Australian fiction. In terms of reception, sexually explicit cues enable the author to optimize the endogenous attention[4] of readers as interest and importance are two key factors correlated to attention. The inclusion of power words such as sexual vocabulary (e.g., "penis," "vagina," "half an erection," "she was aroused," "I entered her," "I had my first orgasm," "cock," "fucking," to take a few examples from *The Americans, Baby*) or any other words and phrases conjuring sexual imagery (*AB*: "love-making," "Do you want to go to bed with me?", "that physical expression of this love," "The ecstasy of nude bodies") are instrumental in captivating and harnessing the reader's attention. This is largely explained by the fact that curiosity drives reward-guided activity in the dopaminergic circuit which affords motivation for learning, but also for food, money and sex, according to cognitive neuroscientist Stanislas Dehaene and colleagues. In other words, sex and curiosity share the same neural pathways in the reward system which generates positively valenced emotions (Dehaene et al. 111). In this respect, sexual references in a literary text get the reader's conscious attention because it is either deemed pleasurable or interesting, thus turning into sexual stimuli.

These power words, which are to be found equally in Moorhouse's, Jaivin's, and Purcell's fiction, have a strong emotional anchor which trigger *arousal* (a term also used in research as a byword for interest) in readers. Sexually explicit cues are responsible for what is known as "attentional capture,"[5] which is mainly caused by emotional stimuli. While molecular biologist John Medina notes that "the brain continuously scans the sensory horizon, with events constantly assessed for their potential interest or importance" (Medina 76), he also explores the reciprocity of this principle. Medina goes on to show how marketing strategies have aptly used this technique, which consists of creating interest through channeled attention. This is all the truer as emotionally arousing elements are more likely to remain in people's memory than ordinary or neutral ones. When discussing our "sexiest brain bits," neuropsychologist Dr. Amee Baird reminds readers that the amygdala "plays a crucial role in processing our emotions, and abuts the hippocampus, which is critical for memory," and concludes that the close proximity of these two structures in the brain would account for the fact "that memories and emotions are closely intertwined [...]" (Baird 13).

Literary pornography enjoyment and sexual arousal are natural pleasures which, thanks to the role played by the nucleus accumbens (also known as the reward center), are neurobiologically inscribed in our capacity to survive as a species. The nucleus accumbens "is heavily connected with pleasure, reinforcement learning, reward seeking, and impulsivity" (Love et al. 394). The reward system comprises the

> amygdala (positive and negative emotions, emotional memory), hippocampus (processing and retrieval of long term memories), and the frontal cortex ([which] coordinates and determines behavior). Taken together, the reward system and its connecting regions modulate, among other things, pleasure, reward, memory, attention, and motivation.
>
> (Love et al. 394)

Sexual arousability is therefore triggered by the combination of four components, which are cognitive, emotional, physiological, and motivational. Put simply, literary attention and neural response to sexually explicit cues pander to people's instinctual and biological needs. However, the influence of literary pornographic exposure seems to be a gender-specific trait as it is more likely to impact women who, according to research, are greater consumers of *literary* pornography than men, who are rather greater consumers of *visual* pornography (Goldsmith et al. 5).

Conclusion

The works under consideration are sexually explicit narratives published in the last 50 years, by writers who have developed their distinct voices while contributing to the normalization of sex in Australian fictional texts. Obviously, it all started with the countercultural group of Balmain writers whose sex-laden stories paved the way for upcoming generations of writers like Linda Jaivin, Justine Ettler, Petra Spear, Christos Tsiolkas, and John Purcell, who would unashamedly exhibit carnal love in their narratives, be they part of mainstream genres such as grunge fiction or of more specialized areas of literature such as erotic fiction and pornography. It thus becomes apparent that the 1970s, which gave momentum to the Australian sexual revolution in print, encapsulate the pivotal decade for representations of sexualities in Australian fiction.

As far as literary reception is concerned, there is no denying that Moorhouse, Jaivin, and Purcell consciously or unconsciously tried to maximize public attention with licentious content by turning creative texts into erogenous zones. These sexually explicit cues are not so much concerned with eliciting sexual arousal as with channeling the literary attention of readers and whetting their appetite for text through an erotics of reading. If these authors were to be called *libertines*, it would be in keeping with the etymology of the word. In other words, rather than seeing them as dissolute writers, one could envisage them as *emancipated* writers, freethinkers who broke free of the conventional rules of staid literary narratives.

Notes

1 The discontinuous narrative concept was inspired from Christina Stead's *The Salzburg Tales* (1934), which linked the stories of various independent characters. Although it is difficult to consider Frank Moorhouse's fiction before 1993 as novels because the author repudiates the genre by assimilating his earlier works to "discontinuous narratives," it is fair to say that his *Conference-Ville* stories have the continuity of action and characters inherent to novelistic plot-lines. However, readers of *The Americans, Baby: A Discontinuous Narrative of Stories and Fragments*, who are already cognizant with Moorhouse's erotics of writing, might be disappointed in *Conference-Ville*, which has a much less pronounced saucy vein. The precious few mentions of sex include a colleague discussing the sexual fantasies of his wife with the narrator, the rekindling of a past sexual affair, and a massage with a hand job given by a sex worker.

2

This chapter is concerned with pornography that achieves what I shall consider its primary effect, sexual arousal, in part by representing a certain kind of norm-breaking: the violation of social or moral norms about sexual behaviour. I call this kind of pornography transgressive pornography. This breaking of norms is a feature in much pornography, both popular and literary – [...]. Such pornography includes scenarios featuring couplings deemed by society inappropriate to various degrees: sex between strangers, sex in public places, sex that transgresses professional ethics, sex between members of different social classes, between members of different age groups, incest, sexual violence, bestiality and so on.

(Newall 206)

3 With the exception of chapter 29 explicitly entitled "Sorry, but It's Too Hot in Here for Clothes" (*GP* 198–201, 210–211) and chapter 32, "He Couldn't Tell" (*GP* 210–211).

4

> So endogenous attention involves focussing your attention on something because the desire to do so comes from within you – you focus on it because you want to. Endogenous attention is sometimes also called *top-down attention*, because the inclination to focus attention is coming from the upper level of the brain's hierarchy of desires: Your conscious wishes.
>
> (Baird 196)

5 "Attentional capture is defined as the phenomenon in which attention is involuntarily directed towards a target stimulus based on the characteristics of that stimulus" (Ono and Taniguchi 26).

Works Cited

Baird, Amee. *Sex in the Brain: How Your Brain Controls Your Sex Life*. Sydney: New South Publishing, 2019.

Dehaene, Stanislas, Yann Le Cun, and Jacques Girardon. *La plus belle histoire de l'intelligence. Des origines aux neurones artificiels: vers une nouvelle étape de l'évolution*. Paris: Robert Laffont, 2018.

Doornwaard, Suzan M., Regina J.J.M. van den Eijnden, Adam Johnson, and Tom F.M. ter Bogt. "Exposure to Sexualized Media Content and Selective Attention for Sexual Cues: An Experimental Study." *Computers in Human Behaviour* 41 (2014): 357–364.

Freud, Sigmund. *Three Essays on the Theory of Sexuality. The 1905 Edition*. London: Verso, 1996.

Goldsmith, Kaitlyn, Cara Dunkley, Silvain Dang, and Boris Gorzalka. "Pornography Consumption and its Association with Sexual Concerns and Expectations Among Young Men and Women." *The Canadian Journal of Human Sexuality* 26 (2017): 1–12.

Jaivin, Linda. *Eat Me*. Melbourne: Text Publishing Company, 1995.

———. "Linda Jaivin on 'Grunge Unplugged'." *Australian Book Review* 177 (1995–1996): 29–30.

Laplanche, Jean, and Jean-Bertrand Pontalis. *Vocabulaire de la psychanalyse*. Paris: Presses Universitaires de France, 1967.

Love, Todd, Christian Laier, Matthias Brand, Linda Hatch, and Raju Hajela. "Neuroscience of Internet Pornography Addiction: A Review and Update." *Behavioral Sciences* 5.3 (2015): 388–433.

Medina, John. *Brain Rules: 12 Principles for Surviving and Thriving at Work, Home, and School*. Melbourne: Scribe, 2008.

Moorhouse, Frank. *The Americans, Baby: A Discontinuous Narrative of Stories and Fragments*. Sydney: Angus and Robertson, 1972.

———. *Conference-Ville*. Sydney: Angus and Robertson, 1976.

Newall, Michael. "An Aesthetics of Transgressive Pornography." *Art and Pornography: Philosophical Essays*. Ed. Hans R.V. Maes and Jerrold Levinson. Oxford: Oxford UP, 2012. 206–228.

Ono, Yohei, and Yasutomi Taniguchi. "Attentional Capture by Emotional Stimuli: Manipulation of Emotional Valence by the Sample Pre-Rating Method." *Japanese Psychological Research* 59.1 (2017): 26–34.

Pasini, Willy. *La Force du désir*. Trans. Jacqueline Henry. Paris: Odile Jacob, 1999.

Pons, Xavier. "Erotic Writing in Australia – Then and Now." *Changing Geographies: Essays on Australia*. Ed. Susan Ballyn, Geoff Belligoi, Kathy Firth, Elisa Morera de la Vall, and Bill Phillips. Barcelona: Centre d'Estudis Australians, Universitat de Barcelona, 2001. 269–277.

Purcell, John. *The Girl on the Page*. Sydney: Fourth Estate, 2018.

Vernay, Jean-François. "Sex in the City: Sexual Predation in Contemporary Australian Grunge Fiction." *AUMLA: Journal of the Australasian Universities Language and Literature Association* 107 (2007): 145–158.

———. *La séduction de la fiction*. Paris: Hermann, 2019.

6   Brains in Pain and Coping Bodies

Trauma, Scars, Wounds, and
the Mind–Body Relationship in
Western Australia Aboriginal
Literature

Introduction

By examining Doris Pilkington Garimara's *Follow the Rabbit-Proof Fence* (1996) and Claire Coleman's *Terra Nullius* (2017), two best-selling literary narratives by contemporary Aboriginal writers born in Western Australia, I shall analyze the relationship between body and mind in the face of vulnerability and despair. Through radically different approaches, these Aboriginal counter-discourses give a central place to the nefarious impact of colonization on Indigenous communities while exploring the latter's responses in cognate areas such as emotional or physical trauma, self-harm, and memory scarring.

In this chapter, I will eschew questions of testimony, agency, truth, and historiography as well as questions of fact versus fiction, of interpretive narrative versus chronicle narrative (Rosanne Kennedy 118), because my prime concern is to focus on the aesthetic representations of mind and body in contemporary Aboriginal literature, regardless of truth valuation issues. I shall first explore the traumatic scenes involving self-injury in Garimara's bio-memoir and then analyse the vulnerable and depressed characters portrayed in Coleman's dystopian novel. My thesis, discussed in the final section, is that Aboriginal authors tend to show in their writings an intuitive understanding of the close interaction between mind and body which bypasses the misguided mind–body Cartesian dualism that Western societies have been endorsing and embracing for centuries.

Brains in Pain: Grief, Trauma, and Self-Injurious Behavior in *Follow the Rabbit-Proof Fence*

Written by historian Nugi Garimara (also known as Doris Pilkington), Molly Craig's daughter, *Follow the Rabbit-Proof Fence* recounts the

DOI: 10.4324/9781003161455-9

ordeal three mixed-descent Mardudjara girls experienced as part of the Stolen Generation. These tweenagers were the victims of a child removal policy that was implemented in the first decade of the twentieth century to forcibly assimilate mixed-race Aboriginal children into Australian society:

> Their removal was arranged by A.O. Neville, the Chief Protector of Aborigines in Western Australia. Guided by notions of white superiority and a pseudo-scientific discourse of eugenics, he developed policies to assimilate and "absorb" Aborigines of mixed decent into the white population and thereby eradicate Aboriginal culture.
>
> (Rosanne Kennedy 165)

Snatched away from their families and relocated to the Moore River Native Settlement by August 1931, Molly, Daisy and Gracie ultimately decamped from the settlement which, in their eyes, presented itself under the traits of a prison, and walked barefoot all the way back along the rabbit-proof fence to their native region, Jigalong, so as to be reunited with their families.

Nugi Garimara reframes the Stolen Generation along with the racist, eugenic, and assimilationist policies of the Australian Government within the larger context of Australia's dark colonial history. These cruel designs enforced in Western Australia by Chief Protector of Aborigines A.O. Neville (referred to as "Devil/Mr Devil" in Claire Coleman's *Terra Nullius*) come across as an ongoing project to spoliate, disempower, exploit, weaken, and ultimately eradicate the *ab origine* custodians of the land:

> Driven off their traditional lands, the Aboriginal people of all areas (except the Central and Western Desert regions) became a dispossessed and devastated race. The people discovered, too late, that the white invaders were human beings and not spirits. The colonists took advantage of the Aboriginal cultural beliefs to further their own gains. The Nyungar people who once walked tall and proud, now hung their head in sorrow. [...] Their pain and suffering remained hidden and repressed, silent and deep.
>
> (*Follow the Rabbit-Proof Fence (FRPF)* 16)

The last sentence of the paragraph, which points to some form of internalized grief ("hidden and repressed, silent and deep"), foregrounds to some extent the psychological fragilization of the Noongar people.

Yet, the book scene which is most revealing of how a state of mind can have a direct impact on the body is when Constable Riggs – bearing the ironical title of "Protector of Aborigines" – comes to take Molly, Daisy, and Gracie away in order to provide them with formal education at the Moore River Native Settlement:

> Molly and Gracie sat silently on the horse, tears streaming down their cheeks as Constable Riggs turned the big bay stallion and led the way back to the depot. A high pitched wail broke out. The cries of agonised mothers and the women, and the deep sobs of grandfathers, uncles and cousins filled the air. Molly and Gracie looked back just once before they disappeared through the river gums. Behind them, those remaining in the camp found strong sharp objects and gashed themselves and inflicted wounds to their heads and bodies as an expression of their sorrow.
>
> (*FRPF* 44–45)

Beyond the rich lexical field of emotive language ("a high pitched wail," "cries," agonized," "the deep sobs," "as an expression of their sorrow"), which a European critic has associated to "universal codes" "conveying grief and despair" (Dorothee Klein 599), we are presented with a rare instance of traumatic grief in Aboriginal literature, one which is associated not with the actual death of a loved one, but with their metaphorical death. Indeed, traumatic grief is classically defined as

> a severe form of separation distress that usually occurs following the sudden and unexpected death of a loved one. Numbness and shock are frequently accompanied by a sense of futility and the meaninglessness of life, although the total syndrome includes many other painful and dysfunctional responses.
>
> (see American Psychological Association)

Faced with the intense emotional pain of having one's child unexpectedly and permanently removed, the male and female adults in the Noongar community have had recourse to self-injury, ultimately scarring themselves as a result of self-inflicted penetrating trauma. But one could wonder if trauma[1] is too strong a word and whether it has been used too loosely in the present situation. As Rosanne Kennedy has it, the discourse of trauma has high relevance in this specific child removal policy context, although it has also been occasionally instrumentalized for various reasons.

In the context of the Stolen Generations, *the discourse of trauma has been used to describe real distress, both emotional and physical,* to convey the damage that has been done by misguided policies, to mount a moral campaign for an apology, to invite empathy, and to legitimate claims for reparation.

(Rosanne Kennedy 123, italics mine)

Dorothee Klein argues that although non-Indigenous readers are "invited to sympathize with the Aboriginal community by drawing on our own experience of what it feels to lose a loved one," "there are limits to our empathy. The custom of inflicting wounds, for instance, remains strange to us as the text can only provide the signifiers; the ultimate meaning, however, will remain inevitably obscure as it is culturally bound" (Dorothee Klein 599). In this very context, while traumatic grief can be construed as a way "to convey the damage that has been done by misguided policies, to mount a moral campaign for an apology, [...] and to legitimate claims for reparation," it can hardly be seen as a narrative strategy "to invite empathy" because of the sheer unfamiliarity the self-harm response would generate in the non-Indigenous readership.

A second scene in that same chapter reinforces the agony of the distressed family members in the eyes of readers and prolongs their exposure to this traumatic moment. It also stresses the unbearable nature of the mother's overwhelming sense of grief and how the pain has been mentally shared by the other distraught members of the community:

Grace's mother, old Granny Friend and other relations in the camp began to wail and cry.

"Worrah, Worrah! He take 'em way, my grannies [granddaughters]," wailed the old lady, as she bent down with great difficulty and picked up a billy can and brought it down heavily on her head. She and the rest of the women began to wail louder, their hearts now burdened with sadness of the girls' departure and the uncertainty of ever seeing them again.

(*FRPF* 48)

It is only in the final chapter entitled "What Happened to Them? Where Are They Now?" – acting as an epilogue of sorts – that readers are given a sketchy cultural explanation of this self-injurious behavior with an additional example proving that these "self-inflicted wounds" are no singular or isolated phenomenon, but rather "a customary action of the distressed and the anguished and a common expression of grief and despair" (*FRPF* 131).

While there is no denying that the author of *Follow the Rabbit-Proof Fence* is depicting as accurately as she can the first-hand traumatic experiences the Mardudjara girls and their family went through without having lived them, it is not impossible that Nugi Garimara could be affected by intergenerational trauma, and most specifically historical trauma, namely her mother's and grandmother's traumas which have been transferred from one generation to the next. Historical trauma is succinctly defined as

> multigenerational trauma experienced by a specific cultural, racial or ethnic group. It is related to major events that oppressed a particular group of people because of their status as oppressed, such as slavery, the Holocaust, forced migration, and the violent colonisation of Native Americans.
>
> (see Administration for Children and Families)

Mutatis mutandis, it therefore also applies to the violent colonization of Indigenous Australians and to the Stolen Generation victims. Although *Follow the Rabbit-Proof Fence* is a discursively mediated testimony of the Stolen Generation, it could still be seen as a case study of scriptotherapy by a subject affected by intergenerational trauma. Caught up in the residues of past emotional trauma by reconstructing her mother's and aunt's painful past, Nugi Garimara would – by wording this account – be experiencing first-hand the therapeutic value of literature. As Paul Armstrong reminds us, stories are double-edged swords and their impact on the human brain/body varies on a continuum ranging from the negative to the positive:

> Stories can have noxious as well as beneficial moral consequences, fueling conflict and violence or promoting empathy and compassion. Narratives can reinforce boundaries between us and them, or they can challenge prevailing conceptions of justice and injustice and encourage democratic conversation about reconfiguring our sense of responsibility toward others.
>
> (Paul Armstrong 207)

What is most fascinating in this nonfiction account is the way acute mental distress finds a dramatic corporeal expression through physical damage (i.e., essentially harming and ultimately scarring oneself) combined with traumatization whose damaging effects are passed from the trauma-affected survivors on to the next generations. *Terra Nullius*, the speculative fiction that I will now turn to, offers different illustrations of how the body and mind are intricately connected.

Coping Bodies: Scars and Sadness as Signs of Vulnerabilities in *Terra Nullius*

In an author's note at the end of her debut novel, Claire Coleman acknowledges – among other sources – the influence of the works of fellow Aboriginal Western Australian writers such as Sally Morgan's *My Place*, Kim Scott's *Benang*, and Doris Pilkington Garimara's *Follow the Rabbit-Proof Fence*. It therefore comes as no surprise to the readers that the Aboriginal people in *Terra Nullius*, similar to that in Nugi Garimara's true-to-life story, is consensually depicted as a spiritually, psychologically, and physically "broken" people. The vulnerable self topos runs like a leitmotif in Aboriginal literature and was first introduced in contact-history novels sympathetic to Indigenous cultures by non-Indigenous novelist Colin Johnson (also known as Mudrooroo).[2] In *Terra Nullius*, the first physical depiction of the male protagonist Jacky Barna (also known as Jacky Jerramungup), who is frantically running away from something (an internment camp) as much as he is running in search of something (home), is hardly laudatory:

> His muscles and his scars, his body made of barbed wire and leather, betrayed that his life has not been easy. A young man, not much more than a teen, he was scarred like an old soldier. He had a young face, if you could see past the habitual look of pain that belonged on the features of a much older man. Nevertheless, his back and limbs were straight. His agony had the aura of something more emotional than physical.
>
> (*Terra Nullius* (*TN*) 7)

The physical damage (essentially scars) visible on Jacky's body is but a mere reflection, indication, and extension of his inner turmoil encapsulated by two words: emotional agony.

In these creative writing narratives segueing into historical realism, early contact time with the various waves of British settlers and the ensuing colonial settlement are systematically presented as the starting point of "the decline of Aboriginal society." A chapter that bears this latter phrase as a title in *Follow the Rabbit-Proof Fence* makes this political statement explicit: "The Nyungar people, and indeed the entire Aboriginal population, grew to realise what the arrival of the European settlers meant for them: it was the destruction of their traditional society and the dispossession of their lands" (*FRPF* 13). Similar claims are made in *Terra Nullius*, a novel which shares the political potency one finds in – and between the lines of – most Aboriginal writings, fiction and nonfiction alike:

> He had learnt, through his friends, that the bent, broken drugged and drunk state of those surviving near the settlements was not the habitual state of Natives. The truth was, it was a sort of depression brought on by what they had lost, brought on by being dominated and controlled by another people. Who could not be depressed, being treated like animals in a land that had once been theirs alone?
>
> (*TN* 83)

In the first section of this speculative dystopian novel sharply divided into two sets of chapters (1–9/10–21), Claire Coleman's omniscient narrator gets to occasionally portray the Noongar people and more often than not stresses their vulnerability. These unflattering descriptions negatively connote the Noongar community, which seems to suffer from some form of chronic depression. It even comes to the point where this weakening condition becomes lethal to their members: "The Natives were always sickly and weak anyway, so it was expected that several would die every year, even every week" (*TN* 67). One can detect a ring of fatalism in these melancholic and nosographic depictions of Aboriginal people which are shown – quite emphatically through the magnifying lens of the dystopian genre – to be experiencing what is nothing short of a living nightmare. As Samantha Lejeune cogently argues, "Coleman's parallels between the reality of British invasion and the dystopian experience prove to the reader that Aboriginal people are living in their own post-apocalyptic world" (Samantha Lejeune 2).

The adjective "broken," which is used a few times in *Terra Nullius* (43/83/103/107/157-8/160), is actually interesting to analyze and deserves close scrutiny. While the term primarily refers to physical damage, it is often used by Claire Coleman in its metaphorical sense, that is in application to the Aboriginal people, by designating individuals who have given up all hope: "He had seen humans with broken hearts, broken minds, in the Native camp near the settlement. They paced slowly and aimlessly, no energy, no direction. Jacky recognised the first signs of their soulless walk in his own" (*TN* 160). The above quote gives us an accurate depiction of how the adjective "broken" is used as an indicator pointing to a specific multifaceted psychopathological syndrome: depression associated with colonization-related cultural trauma. The emotional state of Indigenous Australians portrayed in *Terra Nullius* is pervasively dominated by images of depression,[3] of ingrained sadness, all of which participate in a continual narrative process underscoring the ablation of hope. This esperectomic streak, which runs throughout this invasion novel, highlights the long-term impact on the Aboriginal people's mind of this aggressive colonization; and denotative language – such as mentioning the "bleak hopeless look on Jacky's face" (*TN* 203) – is obviously Claire Coleman's preferred stylistic device to expose the harmful psychological and physiological effects of colonization on her people. This overall picture of despair and damaged souls one gets from reading *Follow the Rabbit-Proof Fence* and *Terra Nullius* translates into a basic equation: weakened minds beget weakened bodies.

The Mind–Body Nexus: Mental Scars and Physical Damage in Aboriginal Literature

In its own way, each book under scrutiny is a literary space of resistance shedding light on past and present (and, in the case of *Terra Nullius*, future) colonial forces of oppression whose impactful traces are visible on scarred minds and bodies. Each of these books focuses on different specific post-1788 Aboriginal historical facts: *Follow the Rabbit-Proof Fence* offers a black counter-memory account of the Stolen Generation scandal, while Claire Coleman's speculative dystopia uses her projective imagination to revisit the 1788 colonial invasion episode. None of these stories are an expression of "the wounded storyteller," as both are third-person narrations.[4] Indeed, these narratives bear no resemblance to acquired brain injury memoirs in which narrators are trying to make sense of their newly discovered disabilities and vulnerable selves by processing their pain through words in order to alleviate their suffering. However, these two Noongar stories do deal with the suffering and the vulnerability of individuals, that of the Aboriginal people, and we shall see that the portrayal of their behaviors in *Follow the Rabbit-Proof Fence* and *Terra Nullius* aptly illustrates mind–body interaction, and more specifically mental causation, defined as "the mind's causal interaction with the world, and in particular, its influence on behaviour" (see David Robb and John Heil).

Aboriginal culture, which has been insulated from the Western philosophical tradition, has not been influenced by Cartesian dualism which posits the body (a material substance, of which brain is part and parcel) and the mind (an immaterial substance) as two separate entities whose interaction is questionable, a cultural perspective which has given rise to what is known as "the mind–body problem" in Western philosophical circles.[5] Neuroscience in the light of contemporary research on consciousness and the mind has another take on this issue and claims to have resolved it. Two notable interventions in this debate in which neuroscience essentially denies the existence of a problem or paradox are Joseph LeDoux, who contends that "You are your synapses," and Sebastian Seung, who claims that "You are your connectome." Traumatic experiences are further evidence of mental causation as they leave traces on both brain and body: mental scars (attested by altered emotional responses) and physical damage.[6] It therefore stands to reason that traumatic experiences scar/rewire the brains of trauma survivors as much as they have a visible impact on their vulnerable bodies and immune systems.

Whether literature helps Claire Coleman and Doris Pilkington Garimara process the residues of historical and cultural trauma is perhaps a side issue, more to do with health than literary studies. What is of paramount importance is to ask ourselves whether denotative language, which Claire Coleman and Doris Pilkington Garimara seem to make exclusive use of, is the most efficient device literature has to translate how trauma affects people. To be sure, these nonfiction and fiction books are by no means instances of psychological realism, which somewhat accounts for the fact that interior characterization (often revealed through interior monologue and flashbacks) has been sacrificed to the engrossing pace of the storytelling. As a result, when foregrounding the action-centered narration through denotation, the *internal* state (i.e., the mental health and lives) of characters can only be revealed through *external* signs of malaise, frailty, and dejection, as exemplified by the excerpts quoted in sections one and two of this chapter. In other words, in terms of Aboriginal literary representations and narrative modes eschewing psychological realism, mental causation translates into an aesthetic strategy because distraught minds can only become visible through the descriptions of affected bodies.

On the one hand, cultural trauma-related plots seem to turn creative writing into political acts of resistance and public awareness campaigns seeking peace-based social change, when factoring in the historical and socio-political contexts. On the other hand, if one is to envisage literary books as "sites of complex ethical enquiry" (Shady Cosgrove 236), the various issues they raise – with sometimes high affective intensity as in the self-harm episode – make readers attuned to questions of ethics and justice in a way that scholarly work covering the same topics might not achieve. The flip side to this literary peace activism is the negatively valenced way Indigenous people represent themselves in literature. Representations of the vulnerable self tend to box in Aboriginal writers by trapping their subaltern positioning in explicit negative stereotyping. The overall effect of depicting Aboriginal corporeality whose integrity has been compromised is perhaps that of a guilt-inducing perspective eliciting concern during the text–reader interaction.

Conclusion

On the surface, as should be clear to readers by now, both texts show the Indigenous people as counter-discursively resistant to the white supremacist ideology and to the colonial power that has violently subjugated First Nations into steady decline. On a deeper level, *Follow the Rabbit-Proof Fence* and *Terra Nullius* subtly reveal the Aboriginal conception of the mind and body relationship. The latter is epitomized by a continuum of sorts on which mental causation sits as part of an aesthetic strategy, whereby the physical bodies of characters become a reading map for their psycho-emotional states – if not symptoms of the tragic consequences of colonization, of human disenfranchisement.

Not only are the authors using fiction as an advocacy platform to voice their grief in the same way Peter Polites and Christos Tsiolkas use fiction in a political fashion to express their moral outrage (see Chapter 8), but their portrayal of the Aboriginal concept of a unitary self is highly pertinent and strikingly at the vanguard of contemporary conceptions of mind–body interaction, as understood by neuroscience. Above all, what Doris Pilkington Garimara and Claire Coleman have achieved is turning the tragedy of living the impact of colonization into living the tragedy of colonization's impact through the reading of their writings.

Notes

1 In her introduction, Anna Thiemann notes that – under the influence of neurocognitivism – "the current paradigm conceives of trauma as an incomprehensible event that is utterly external to the passive yet sovereign human subject." She further adds that current research "claim that traumatic memories are 'unspeakable' [...] because they are stored and experienced as intrusive visceral sensations that cannot be properly communicated and integrated into the history of the psyche" (Anna Thiemann 4).

2 Colin Johnson's *Doctor Wooreddy's Prescription for Enduring the Ending of the World* (1983) and *The Master of the Ghost Dreaming* (1991) are two novels that expose the deleterious effects of White settlement. Like his more poetic work *The Master of the Ghost Dreaming* (1991), *Doctor Wooreddy's Prescription for Enduring the Ending of the World* is a truly postcolonial work fighting the negative effects of colonization by challenging non-Indigenous Australia's official version of contact history with an Indigenous perspective.

3 Sivasankaran Balaratnasingam and Aleksandar Janca call for the reconceptualization of the depression diagnosis for Indigenous populations in the light of their cultural history. They argue to err on the side of caution by opting for a more nuanced cultural approach to diagnosing clinical depression within Indigenous communities given that a 2015 review indicates that the "prevalence rates of major depressive disorder among Indigenous Australians ranged between 4.3% and 51%." They also raise a highly pertinent question: "How does a clinician distinguish the psychological effects of ongoing cultural trauma, racism, poverty, disempowerment and social exclusion – which no doubt increase the likelihood of depression – from a clinical diagnosis of depression?" (Sivasankaran Balaratnasingam and Aleksandar Janca 16.)

4 *Follow the Rabbit-Proof Fence* was written by Molly Craig's daughter, who did not experience first-hand what the three female protagonists of the story went through. Therefore, as the biographer and professional historian acknowledges in her introduction to the book, her narrative of traumatic separation is a synthesis of data collected through "interviews," of "a vivid imagination" (*FRPF* xi), as well as an admixture of "childhood memories" (*FRPF* xii), documented research into archives and a writer's empathic imagination:

> In my mind I walked the same paths and called on my skills as a writer to describe the scenery and how it looked through their eyes. By combining my imagination and the information from records of geographical and botanical explorations undertaken in the area during the 1900s and later, I was able to build a clearer picture of the vegetation and landscape through which the girls trekked.
>
> (*FRPF* xii)

Terra Nullius contains the story of Jacky in third-person narration mode, through the eyes of an omniscient narrator.

5 For a brief introduction of the mind–body problem, see section 2.1 of D. Robb and J. Heil. "What is the Mind–Body Nexus?" *The Stanford Encyclopedia of Philosophy* (Summer 2019 Edition), Edward N. Zalta ed. https://plato.stanford.edu/archives/sum2019/entries/mental-causation/.

6 In *The Body Keeps the Score: Brain, Mind and Body in the Healing of Trauma*, Bessel van der Kolk comes to the conclusion, at the very end of his chapter on "Body–Brain Connections," that "the memory of trauma is encoded in the viscera, in heartbreaking and gut-wrenching emotions, in autoimmune disorders and skeletal/muscular problems" (Bessel van der Kolk 86).

Works Cited

Administration for Children and Families. "Trauma." *Administration for Children and Families.* www.acf.hhs.gov/trauma-toolkit/trauma-concept.

American Psychological Association. "Traumatic Grief." *APA Dictionary of Psychology*. https://dictionary.apa.org/traumatic-grief.

Armstrong, Paul. *Stories and the Brain: The Neuroscience of Narrative*. Baltimore, MD: Johns Hopkins UP, 2020.

Balaratnasingam, Sivasankaran, and Aleksandar Janca. "Depression in Indigenous Australians: Getting it Right." *Medical Journal of Australia* 211.1 (2019): 16–17.

Coleman, Claire. *Terra Nullius*. Sydney: Hachette, 2017.

Cosgrove, Shady E. "Reading for Peace? Literature as Activism – An Investigation into New Literary Ethics and the Novel." *Activating Human Rights and Peace: Universal Responsibility*. Ed. Rob Garbutt. Lismore: Southern Cross University, Centre for Peace and Social Justice, 2008. 223–239.

Johnson, Colin. *Doctor Wooreddy's Prescription for Enduring the Ending of the World*. Melbourne: Hyland House, 1983.

———. *Master of the Ghost Dreaming*. Sydney: Angus & Robertson, 1991.

Kennedy, Rosanne. "Stolen Generations Testimony: Trauma, Historiography, and the Question of 'Truth'." *Aboriginal History* 25 (2001): 116–131.

———. "Vulnerable Children, Disposable Mothers: Holocaust and Stolen Generations Memoirs of Childhood." *Life Writing* 5.2 (2008): 161–184.

Klein, Dorothee. "Narrating a Different (Hi)Story: The Affective Work of Counter-Discourse in Doris Pilkington's *Follow the Rabbit-Proof Fence*." *Interventions: International Journal of Postcolonial Studies* 18.4 (2016): 588–604.

LeDoux, Joseph. *Synaptic Self: How Our Brains Become Who We Are*. London: Macmillan, 2002.

Lejeune, Samantha. "Speculating Reality: A Review of Claire Coleman's *Terra Nullius*." *NEW Emerging Scholars in Australian Indigenous Studies* 5.1 (2020). https://epress.lib.uts.edu.au/student-journals/index.php/NESAIS/article/view/1578/1778.

Pilkington, Doris. *Follow the Rabbit-Proof Fence*. St Lucia: U of Queensland P, 1996.

Robb, David, and John Heil. "Mental Causation." *The Stanford Encyclopedia of Philosophy* (Summer 2019 Edition). Ed. Edward N. Zalta. https://plato.stanford.edu/archives/sum2019/entries/mental-causation/.

Seung, Sebastian. *Connectome: How the Brain's Wiring Makes Us Who We Are*. Boston, MA: Houghton Mifflin Harcourt, 2012.

Thiemann, Anna. *Rewriting the American Soul: Trauma, Neuroscience and the Contemporary Literary Imagination*. London: Routledge, 2019.

van der Kolk, Bessel. *The Body Keeps the Score: Brain, Mind and Body in the Healing of Trauma*. New York, NY: Allen Lane, 2014.

Part IV

Cognition and Emotions

This last section will put the focus on affect studies, moral behavior, and strong emotions such as rage and outrage in creative writing processes and in the cognitive mechanisms of reader-focused reception. The first comparative chapter makes inroads into literary activism and examines the gay fiction by Christos Tsiolkas and Peter Polites with regards to aesthetic manifestations of expressed and repressed rage and how it is encoded in the text. The final discussion on the public reception of a major controversy involving Helen Demidenko will engage affective literary theory by measuring the emotional effect of literary fraud and willful deceit on professional readers and their literary appreciation of an artwork.

DOI: 10.4324/9781003161455-10

7 Angry Gay Men

Rage, Race, and Reward in Contemporary Australian Advocacy Fiction

Introduction

Christos Tsiolkas and Peter Polites can be defined as queer, second-generation Greek Australian creative writers who articulate the triangulation of gay sex, class conflict, and ethnicity in what could be defined as slice-of-life-inspired fictional narratives.[1] Whether fully expressed or suppressed through literary ploys, rage lies at the basis of their stories and takes various literary forms. Tsiolkas' narratives often feature rage-filled protagonists whose social activist views yield rewarding outcomes. Similarly, Peter Polites' unforgiving indictment of Australia being caught up in consumerism and rapacity in *The Pillars* comes across as a vitriolic social critique that seeks cognitive rewards.

By drawing on cognitive literary theory, I shall analyze how Tsiolkas' branding tropes of excessive violence[2] – which transpires through words, thoughts and actions in *Merciless Gods* – and Peter Polites' corrosive satire peppered with bittersweet irony can be construed as aesthetic manifestations of rage. Exploring the cognitive underpinnings of anger may prove illuminating in understanding how Tsiolkas and Polites seek social justice through advocacy literature.

The Politics of Tsiolkas' Expressed Rage: Violence in Words, Thoughts, and Actions in *Merciless Gods*

From Ari's rebelliousness in *Loaded* (1995) to Danny Kelly's frustrated ambitions in *Barracuda* (2013),[3] it is fair to say that a set of strong emotions run as a unifying thread through Christos Tsiolkas' works of fiction whose emotional power has repeatedly been highlighted by critics.[4] One could even argue that Tsiolkas' initial exploration of masculine individualism, dissatisfaction, and aggressiveness in grunge fiction has developed into an underlying leitmotif in his fiction, which

DOI: 10.4324/9781003161455-11

manifests itself as a gender-marked highly inflamed emotion. The Melbourne-based novelist has even used rage – succinctly defined as violent, uncontrollable anger – as the lynchpin of *The Slap*'s pivotal incident in which a young sore loser meets the exasperation of a grown-up.[5] The novelist's violent subject matter (coprophilia, racism, and anti-Semitism) that confronted readers in *Dead Europe* (2005) is taken up again as subtle variations on the same theme in *Merciless Gods* (2014), a collection of short stories which spans over close to two decades of creative writing. However, as I have argued elsewhere, Tsiolkas' repelling topics are hardly gratuitous and even provide fertile terrain to indulge in Freudian readings of his fiction (see Vernay, "The Politics of Desire"). Rather than discussing *Merciless Gods* in psychoanalytical terms, this chapter will make forays into cognitive literary theory to explore the aesthetics and politics of rage with reference to affect studies and cognition.

According to Joseph LeDoux's *The Emotional Brain* (1998), there is no such thing as an isolated phenomenon termed emotion, but rather a diverse range of emotion systems such as the anger system, the fear system, the happiness system, and the unhappiness system. Within the scope of this classification, rage is part and parcel of the anger system, as much as indignation, frustration, fury, choler, irritation, annoyance, resentment, envy, jealousy, ingratitude, and scorn.[6] While rage and other emotions lie at the core of human subjectivity, it is always a challenge to represent them in fiction. Indeed, visual cues are crucial to interpreting emotions that are quintessentially manifesting through nonverbal cues such as body language. Therein lies the ordeal of expressing rage verbally in fiction, in a space where emotions are ancillary to, and thoroughly dependent on, words typed on a blank page bereft of iconography which could reveal facial expressions. Emotions such as rage therefore need to be encoded by the creative writer in the flesh of denotative and connotative words, in a very specific language register, in the expression of violent thoughts, and most obviously in the graphic depiction of violent actions.

Denotation and connotation are used alternatively in the short story entitled "Porn 1," in which a mother enters an X-rated video store to purchase a copy of a blue movie in which her AIDS-infected son Nick, who died in Los Angeles from a drug overdose, features as gay porn star Ricky Pallo. The mother's anger surges crescendo throughout the story, from repressed feelings while browsing through gay pornography for which she "did not allow herself any emotion" to her watching gay porn and being judgmental about the actors, calling them "Whores" (*Merciless Gods* (*MG*) 274, 283). The inclusion of such brutal, derogatory words that connote uncontrollable anger is a somewhat more subtle literary technique reminiscent of the "Show, don't tell" Jamesian mantra. However, the consecution of two strong verbs denoting rage such as "hate" and "detest," with an added dimension of moral judgment transpiring in the second term which denotes disapprobation-based aversion, is also effective to build up tension and translate the mother's escalating anger:

> This was not Nick's body. He had muscles now, his torso and chest were smooth. She rose, began to pace, not looking, looking. He was on his back, the ugly man was sodomising him. She hated him, she detested him.
> "Why?" It was a scream. "You didn't need money. We gave you everything. Why? Why? *Why?*" The choked word was her defence, she threw it at the screen, no longer caring who heard: the neighbours, the laughing children, the whole world. She wanted Nick to hear it, wanted him to understand her fury.
>
> (*MG* 285)

Another linguistic trick to express emotions, and more specifically climaxing rage, is for creative writers to resort to a specific language register, namely vulgar speech. There is no denying that readers have been emotionally impacted by Ari's spectacular hate-filled outburst in *Loaded*, Tsiolkas' debut novel which depicts human susceptibility to radical hatred, xenophobic sentiments, and nihilism:

> The Serb hates the Croat who hates the Bosnian who hates the Albanian who hates the Greek who hates the Turk who hates the Armenian who hates the Kurd who hates the Palestinian who hates the Jew who hates everybody. Everyone hates everyone else, a web of hatred connects the planet.
>
> (*Loaded* (*L*) 64)

The enraged protagonist sees the racism-infested world as "a web of hatred," which can only be untangled through global extermination. The novelist's shrewd inclusion of vulgar words (like "shithole" and "fucked up") is, with regards to the limitations of print publications discussed above,[7] an effective giveaway of Ari's uncontrollable anger:

> Pol Pot was right to destroy, he was wrong not to work it out that you go all the way. You don't kill one class, one religion, one party. You kill everyone because we are all diseased, there is no way out

of this shithole planet. War, disease, murder, AIDS, genocide, holocaust, famine. I can give ten dollars to an appeal if I want to, I can
write a letter to the government. But the world is now too fucked
up for small solutions. That's why I like the idea of it all ending in a
nuclear holocaust. If I had access to the button, I'd push it.

(*L* 64)

Similarly, Tsiolkas' generous use of expletives in *Merciless Gods* has
not gone unnoticed (see Ley). The "Sticks, Stones" narrative is a reminder
of how powerful the cognitive impact of words is, an impact which is
made forceful through emotive language, along with the positive and
negative connotations associated with words. In this respect, the allusion
the short story title makes to "Sticks and stones may break my bones /
But words will never break me" is a biting irony which debunks the
counterintuitive proverbial wisdom behind this popular adage derived
from childhood folklore. Although this saying was initially meant to
downplay the consequences of verbal abuse, it goes against the findings
of research in psychology, which attests to the damaging impact of
verbal bullying (see Dieter Wolke and Suzet Tanya Lereya). In "Sticks,
Stones," Marianne is picking up her son Jack and his friends Billy and
Stavros from school, as part of her car pool duties. She is aware that the
boys have just called Amelia, a socially isolated schoolgirl diagnosed
with Down syndrome, a "mong." The mother is all the more upset
that her son will not apologize and even ragingly mumbles an expletive
when leaving the car: "Bitch. He had called her a bitch. Another word
not supposed to hurt" (*MG* 217). Her husband Rick also minimizes, if
not condones, the incident. It does not take long for Marianne to be
tormented by Jack's unremorseful vilification:

The dirty word kept repeating itself in her head. Mong. Mong.
Mong. Maco. Nigger, slope, bitch and cunt and slut and fag and
poofter and dyke. She did not trust their ease with words that hurt
so much. She refused to believe that they had been exorcised of
their venom and their cruelty.

(*MG* 219)

The association of homophobic ("fag and poofter and dyke"), xenophobic ("Nigger"), and misogynistic ("bitch and cunt and slut") verbal
bullying in the same paragraph, under the pen of a gay writer of Greek
descent, can be construed as a broader comment on the victimiza-
tion of scapegoats and on the long shadow verbal abuse casts over the
victims' lives.

In stories such as "Porn 2," it is unclear as to whether Tsiolkas is exposing the underground forms of violence in gay sadistic sexuality or simply eroticizing violence in the eyes of his gay readership with, in this particular case, a twink-gets-fucked-by-a-monstercock scenario. However, physical violence is seen as being dissociated from rage in this specific short story. Rather, the strong emotion is expressed through the narrator's dark thoughts, which are directed against Dick Cheese Saunders. The latter's offensively ungenerous comment ("The kid's fucking cross-eyed!"), which indicates his rejection of the possibility that the narrator could join his friend Mickey on the gay porn shoot, triggers a strong response in the debased victim, who retaliates by fantasizing Saunders' death:

> I looked down at the floor, humiliated, and then I went spastic, wanting to knife the cunt, but then I remembered what Alex, who was my sponsor at the Congregation, had taught me. He taught me that when I get pissed off, I should just pray, instead of losing it.
>
> (*MG* 292)

Further down the track, after receiving a couple of blows by the brutal movie director, the narrator's mental counter-aggression reaches an unprecedented peak and his murderous impulses are now tinged with sadism:

> I wish I could make people die with my thoughts. I'd make Saunders die a million times, in burning oil, vultures tearing at his innards, a spike up his arse to his throat. I could watch him die a million times.
>
> (*MG* 302–303)

Showing rage with words that graphically depict action with an extreme degree of violence, such as forced coprophilia in the short story entitled "Petals," is another literary ploy to express retaliatory rage in print. The Greek narrator is behind bars, sharing a cell with two other inmates, Tzim and a bully named Stiv Gharin. The imprisoned narrator, who reaches a point of exasperation with Gharin's ongoing physical and verbal acts of aggression, eventually opts for a retributive physical counter-aggression:

> In the latrine I can hear Stiv Gharin pissing a fountain. Then he lets drop a foul fart as he shits. […] I wrap Tzim's cloth around my hand and I dip into the latrine. I grab his three fat shits. […] I am opening his mouth, I am seeing right down to his black heart and

I am grabbing the shit and pushing it all the way down. I am filling his mouth and I am filling his throat. I fill the animal's lungs with the shit.

(*MG* 88–89)

To be sure, the explicit and sometimes graphic manifestations of rage in *Merciless Gods* have a significant emotional impact on readers, who are occasionally thrown into a state of shock, but we shall now see that Peter Polites' narrative techniques, hinting at suppressed rage, may be another way – albeit more subtle – of impacting readers with visually strong literary representations.

The Aesthetics of Polites' Repressed Rage: Literary Representations and Techniques in *The Pillars*

The Pillars is Peter Polites' second fiction book, after the much lauded *Down to Hume* (2017), a queer-noir novel about gay relationships marred by domestic violence. Based in Pemulwuy, an ethnically diverse suburb in Greater Western Sydney, Pano is in a complex cis male gay relationship with Kane, his landlord, sex friend, and secret infatuation. Kane and Pano have the kind of loose relationship that you find in Tsiolkas' narratives: the protagonist's life, whose reliable bedrock is provided by his regular sex partner, is spiced up with random sex, one night stands, and the occasional group sex.

This semi-autobiographical narrative in free indirect speech smacks of the multicultural Australia that has colored the pages of *The Slap*, without having any of the underlying soap opera culture which has facilitated the adaptation of Tsiolkas' internationally acclaimed novel into a successful ABC series. Where Melbourne-born Tsiolkas is concerned with grounding his stories in the working-class suburbia of his hometown, Sydney-born Polites sticks to the impoverished migrant suburbs of Western Sydney. While there are many more commonalities to be found between these two gay creative writers, Polites comes across as a less overtly angry man than Tsiolkas.

On the one hand, readers will come across no misanthropic tirades, no murderous impulses, no character nourishing an all-consuming rage, and no *frequent* coarse language in Polites' second novel. At best, you will find an irritated character like Basil uttering a couple of expletives out of frustration for not being able to get any phone reception: "Fucking river! Fucking trees!" (*The Pillars (P)* 36.) Beyond his literary exploitation of emotive language, the novelist is also making a characterization-inflected statement. By hinting at Basil's disrespect for the environment and his greedy need to make business at all costs, he is chiefly depicting him *obliquo ductu* as an unethical, narcissistic businessman. On the other hand, readers are exposed to name-calling and other forms of bullying, such as a Kubrick-like scene of bashing towards the end of *The Pillars*. Racism is also occasionally dealt with.

According to journalist Con Stamocostas, Polites admitted "that the fuel for his second novel contained an element of rage," without specifying the reasons for it:

> "This book starts from a place of anger," [Polites] revealed. "But I'm not going to lie, I enjoyed writing this novel more than my first book *Down the Hume* because I put so much comedy into it. Part of the comedy is outright slapstick and the other part is satire in the traditions of Henry James or Brett Easton Ellis and how they satirise class. I wanted to satirise the lower middle classes and their aspirations."[8]

Peter Polites deploys pop culture-flavored comedy (which I wouldn't characterize as "slapstick") and satire as modes of expression that enable him to channel the narrator's pent-up anger and reveal the (actual or fantasied) savagery behind the veneer of civility in contemporary society which, according to Pano's mother – who is also prone to exaggeration – is on the brink of collapse:

> Before Mum's brain became a beanbag, she taught me that the threat of a battle or a slight tremor in the economy could make society crumble. She prophesied that one day, while we all waited in line for skim caramel lattes, the stock markets would take a dip and hydrochloric acid would be flung in our faces. [...] Don't worry about the fact that you will never be able to afford a home. Worry about the economy shredding! That's when they will all come, with their black shirts and bayonets, and then you will see the drowned bodies and slit necks. And I would stand there and say, "But Mum, why are you telling me this when I'm ten years old?"
>
> *(P 6–7)*

With a keen eye for details, Peter Polites presents with a vitriolic social critique of Australia's consumerism and culture of greed. His portrayal of a corrupt society exposes the threat to the younger generations who are deprived of having the possibility to afford a home in Sydney's highly artificially inflated real estate market:

> I stopped at the window of Vas Bros Real Estate and looked at all the apartments for sale, trying to find the logic in a two-bedroom apartment in Bankstown selling for half a million dollars. There were professional photos of men in polyester suits holding gravels and standing outside houses. A human-sized decal of a balding man in his finest suit with dental-work smile grinned at me like I wasn't in on the joke.
>
> > (*P* 19)

By foregrounding social advancement and materialistic success in his story of modern-day Australia, Peter Polites is probing the deep-rooted insecurity that underlies this misguided ethnic aspirationalism. His unforgiving indictment of Australia being caught up in consumerism and rapacity is to some extent reminiscent of David Williamson's satirical plays such as *The Emerald City* (1987) and *Up for Grabs* (2000), but perhaps brought to a higher cynical pitch in the final chapters of his tale, one which ethical readers might find unsettling.

In *The Pillars*, satire is not as much a genre as a literary device based on humor, situational irony (discussed hereafter), and a degree of exaggeration germane to caricature. The author's stereotypical representations, which affect any area of existence, do not seem to be primarily politically driven or focused. Rather, they instate Peter Polites as a fledgling sociologist or social commentator, as illustrated in chapter 12 with a humorous analysis of the social codes inherent to the corporate pecking order and, a few short pages later, with the mechanics of gay sexual intercourse comically described as "more experimental opera than sex; I expected the door to open and two nude figures in goat masks to come out and dance around a yellow hazard sign" (*P* 80).

Despite Pano being an obscure poet, he has been given a chance to earn a living through his creative writing skills by ghost writing the life story of his high school friend, Basil. The latter is a straight self-made entrepreneur who has expanded the construction company his father managed until retirement. Basil's characterization in chapter 4 probably exemplifies the novelist's bittersweet irony at its best:

> He was one of the first boys in our school to have the hair waxed from his legs, claiming all athletes did it. Later, he was a trailblazer for the young male dogs by using an experimental new laser treatment to remove all his body hair. In our last year of high school, I overheard him talking about how important natural beauty was to him, which

was why he didn't bang wog girls, because they spent too much time on themselves.

(*P* 21)

In this excerpt, Polites uses situational irony (as opposed to verbal irony and dramatic irony), which, in this instance, rests on the discordance between what is expected (Basil would naturally be associating with body-conscious girls who spend a lot of time and money on their image) and what actually turns out to be (Basil is valuing natural beauty and rejecting girls who spend as much time as him taking care of their looks).

The unavowed will to implement social change through satire and irony (for Polites) or through enraged characters and graphic depictions of excessive violence (for Tsiolkas) partakes of advocacy literature that offers cognitive rewards while agitating for social justice through the exploitation of strong emotions like rage, outrage, anger, and disgust.

Advocacy Literature: Anger, Social Injustice, Outrage, and Cognitive Reward

The expression or repression of rage as a defining trait of male authors from ethnic backgrounds with working-class affinities like Polites and Tsiolkas squares well with Sue Kim's cognitive literary analysis of anger, and especially with the opening paragraphs of her monograph *On Anger: Race, Cognition, Narrative*. In her own words,

Anger may be partly physiological, cognitive, and psychological, yet it is also deeply ideological, inseparable from factors such as race, class, gender, sexuality, ethnicity, nation, and religion. We see cultural and ideological configurations of anger in a variety of ways: People of colour are either more or less angry than white people. A man's anger expresses, while constituting, his masculinity, while a woman's anger is anti-feminine. The middle class defines and identifies itself through "control" of emotions and against the uncontrolled emotions of both the wealthy and the poor.

(1)

The fact that we, readers, are observing the manifestations of repressed rage mediated through literary ploys such as irony and satire is every bit as relevant to understanding why Peter Polites' rage is more subdued than Tsiolkas'. Irony, as a general rule, tones down the aggressiveness and threat perceived in a more straightforward negative criticism and relies on the ability to interpret social cues through what is generally called theory of mind.[9] While the criticism that lies behind remains negative, irony comes across as more socially acceptable because it is couched in a more roundabout way, even though its comprehension requires more cognitive effort than any straightforward negative criticism. While, like sarcasm, satire could be defined as humor and wit born of repressed anger, it differs from it in so far as satire is constructive (unlike sarcasm, which is aggressively destructive) and turns out to be a subtle eye-opener for audiences.

Anger is an object-directed emotion like contempt, hatred, and indignation, and therefore implies the representation of an object. In other words, individuals are angry at a specific object[10] whose target could be an individual, a collective like society, or a concept such as social injustice, wrongdoing, harm-doing, to name a few. Clustering as two of the six basic emotions in Paul Ekman's initial taxonomy (wrath, grossness, sacredness, joy, loneliness, and shock), which he eventually expanded in the 1990s, anger and disgust are often amalgamated as forms of indignation when it comes to expressing moral outrage. However, as discussed in the next chapter, anger and disgust are to be dissociated on a functional level because anger is mainly manifesting itself through direct aggression (such as physical violence and verbal abuse at the moral violator) while disgust is rather associated with indirect aggression.

More often than not, Tsiolkas' use of direct aggression and dialectical anger in *Merciless Gods* is not motivated by initial aggression, or frustration like Danny's rage in *Barracuda*, but rather with counter-aggression, which comes as an affective response to socio-political or interpersonal factors. In Tsiolkas' world of a thousand shades of gray, there is no room for Manichean solutions. In "Sticks, Stones," Marianne will soon find out that if she lives up to her principles of social justice, she might strain her relationship with her beloved son Jack and even with her partner Rick. Therefore, maintaining strong personal ethics – in a complex world where multiple paradigms should be factored in – becomes an intractable problem for idealists who wish to embark on a Quixotic quest for absolutes.

Each with their distinctive mode underpinned by anger, Tsiolkas and Polites are using fiction as an effective advocacy platform to voice their moral indignation at the lurking evils that plague contemporary Australian society: homophobia, racism, social inequality, neo-liberalism, rampant materialism, superficiality, conflicts,[11] to name a few.

Freudian psychoanalysis teaches us that when individuals are bottling up their feelings, a range of consequences is to be expected: either their repressed feelings find themselves sublimated or, at some point, the subject will ultimately be confronted by the return of the repressed. Failing any of these two options, the unsublimated repression of feelings will become toxic for the physical and mental health of the subject (see Patel and Patel). As it is socially unacceptable to express one's rage in public, rage is bound to be sublimated and find its indirect manifestations in published works of creative writing. Through fiction, made public at the end of the publishing process, rage not only becomes socially acceptable but also takes on as many discursive forms as possible – ranging from showing the shocking brutality and obscenity of transgressive scenes infused with racism, homophobia, misogyny and blasphemy to the more distanced caricatured account of how imperfect our world is.

What fiction teaches us is that anger, while often being misunderstood as an intrinsically negative social emotion due to its impulsivity and capacity to cloud reason, can also have short- or long-term benefits. Its most direct impact for authors is cognitive reward: the sublimated emotion into rage-filled or satiricized narratives allows literary advocates to transpose and reorganize the imperfect real world into fictional space in order to right the perceived wrongs through fantasy-filled scenarios and to raise awareness by bringing vexed issues in the limelight. Like playfulness in childhood, writing allows Tsiolkas and Polites "free organization of the fantasies of their desire"[12] as well as the exploitation of make-believe in a transitional space where inner and outer worlds coexist and where rage, irony, and satire have the potential to become pleasurably retaliatory.[13] As for the long-term benefits, some readers might be subtly goaded towards social change. For instance, chapter 29 of *The Pillars* will force readers to witness a violent gay-bashing scene:

> A semicircle of teens around me. Who you been looking at? Why you been looking at people in the dark? Faggot! Creep! Weirdo! Step up to me. Ball fists. Cover my head with my arms. Cover my ears. What's it like being watched faggot!
>
> Fist connects with left side of my head, keel to the side, shoulder hits ground. Roll onto face. Pull knees under torso. Turn into a ball. Foot kicks my side. Oh, you wanna see us naked? Fingernails tear shirt, fingernails tear shorts, fingernails rip clothes to ribbons. [...] Arms rain on me. Legs kick my flank. [...] Direct blows onto my arms. Shoes wounds my side. One of them puts his foot on my back. Pushes me down. Closer to the ground, compressed. I hear camera

phones taking photos of me as someone stands on my back because he wants a trophy shot.

(P 210)

This *Clockwork Orange*-inspired scene of violence whose mental visualization might shock readers could also sensitize empathetic citizens to the persecution of minority groups. Naturally, this show-don't-tell mode is more impactful on readers than a gay-bashing episode told in "reported action,"[14] the intellectualization-based mode Tsiolkas used in his eponymous short story. The narrator of "Merciless Gods" recounts the gay-bashing of a middle-aged man in a public toilet known to be a gay beat. The young perpetrator got away with "a suspended sentence" for his hideous crime chiefly because he argued that he was solicited, therefore his murderous impulse was seen as a counter-aggression:

> Not long after Mark had first moved into the flat, a middle-aged man was viciously bashed in one of the cubicles. When he was discovered, he was in a coma, a sleep from which he never recovered. The police found his killer, a young father in his twenties [...]. It could have been me, [Mark] would always say, I used to go across to that beat on a weekly basis, it could have been me bashed and left dying on that concrete slab, it could have been me that bastard punched and kicked and pissed on. In the end, the killer pleaded guilty manslaughter with diminished responsibility. It may seem strange now that such a cruel crime could lead to such a verdict, but it occurred at a time when sexual minorities had not long been demanding a space within mainstream culture; and the law, being the law, being slow and cautious, took pity on a father.

(MG 21–22)

What sounds like empathy on Mark's behalf is a mere identification process, because Mark seems to be more concerned about what could have happened to him numerous times than what actually happened to the deceased victim. Here again – a classical trait in Tsiolkas' fiction – we have an angry *male* character overwhelmed by a moralistic all-consuming rage that courses through him. This time, the character's distress is revealed through what is known as "angry tears," most commonly observed in child behavior (see Seltzer):

> "You have to understand," Mark was saying, "that for the first time in my life I understood what it meant to be outside society. [...] I was a middle-class white kid who had an intellectual understanding of

oppression but I had never felt the outrage of injustice. The man who died was just like me – a little older, sure, but a professional white middle-class guy who happened to be a faggot and, because he was a faggot, his death was permissible." Mark drew a breath and held back his tears.

"If that bastard had apologised once, if just once he had said sorry for what he did, I think anger would have dissipated."

(*MG* 22)

Conclusion

At a general level, my reading of *Merciless Gods* and *The Pillars* confirms Sue Kim's contention that "*Anger is gendered, raced, sexed, classed*" (68).[15] More specifically, what our study of these episodes of rage and corrosive representations reveals is that – whatever the forms of their discursive manifestations – they energetically advocate for social change by visually and cognitively impacting the minds of readers. Tsiolkas' sublimation of rage into creativity can be taken to be the key constituent of the hysterization of rage in his fiction, whereas Polites' sublimation chiefly camouflages rage and tames a socially unacceptable emotion into entertaining sociological views of contemporary Australia. It becomes apparent that all this aggressiveness deviated and channeled through literary devices and techniques is primarily retributive as it brings the authors cognitive reward by alleviating the sense of injustice that human minds are ill-equipped to cope with.

Notes

1 This applies to most of their stories although Tsiolkas' *Dead Europe*, which occasionally segues into the fantastic, would be considered as an exception. I use the phrase "slice-of-life-inspired" because Polites' and Tsiolkas' fictional narratives have many affinities with slice-of-life literature, such as the use of social realism reflecting the language of everyday people, a focus on domesticity and the mundanity of life, faithful depictions of reality, to name a few. However, their stories do have a mild narrative arc with a strong proclivity for moral judgment, as opposed to slice-of-life literature which features open-ended plots whose progress is fairly inconspicuous and shows no inkling of moral judgment.

2 Neil Bartlett has perceptively commented on "Tsiolkas's branding as a professional shocker" in the following excerpt:

> Although it is also the violence in these stories that will strike home on a first reading, and which will doubtless contribute to Tsiolkas's branding as a professional shocker – the graphic unsafe sex, the murders,

suicides and rapes, the humiliating epithets lobbed like grenades – what makes the collection really work is that the trigger moment in a story will release bravery or decency as often as it unleashes savagery.

(see Bartlett)

3   For a perceptive analysis of Danny Kelly's anger and how this anger streak runs through Christos Tsiolkas' œuvre, see Jessica Gildersleeve's *Christos Tsiolkas: The Utopian Vision*:

> In many ways, then, Danny Kelly's violence and anger figure a continuation of the marginalised character of Gary in *The Slap* – one of the few central characters to be refused a focalised chapter of his own – as well as the careless violence of Ari in *Loaded*, the self-torture of Tommy in *The Jesus Man*, and the savage, bloodthirsty aggression of Isaac in *Dead Europe*.
>
> (96)

4   See the book reviews by Neill Bartlett ("Tsiolkas is expert at evoking brutal but often elusive states of rage, grief and bewilderment, and, crucially, at making you wonder where their roots really lie.") and Heather Taylor Johnson ("He writes characters who are fuelled by anger, who do shocking things, whom we somehow recognise in our own selves."). Andrew McCann discusses

> the plights of Tsiolkas's early fictional protagonists (Ari in *Loaded*, Tommy in *The Jesus Man* or Isaac in *Dead Europe*) as embodying a range of emotional and corporeal responses (arousal, anger, hatred, shame) that register their distance from this admittedly hypothetical horizon.
>
> (McCann 6–7)

5   Hugo, one of the kids playing in a typical Melburnian backyard, was frustratingly underperforming at a game of iconic Aussie cricket and started to become difficult. Harry, one of the grown ups gathering at this multicultural suburban party, "lifted the boy up in the air" and then "set him on the ground. The boy's face had gone dark with fury. He raised his foot and kicked wildly in Harry's shin" (*TS* 40).

6   Other neuroscientists who have devised parallel taxonomic categories, perceive the rage system as one of man's seven basic emotional dispositions. The other six basic emotional dispositions are: the seeking system, the fear system, the lust system, the care system, the panic/separation distress system, and the play system (see Antonio Alcaro, Stefano Carta, and Jaak Panksepp).

7   Incidentally, it is worth noting that if *Loaded* were available as an audio book, the perceptible irate tone of voice would make the emotive use of coarse language superfluous.

8   Con Stamocostas, "Peter Polites: 'Mortgage, success, houses, investment. These aren't Greek values.'" *Neo Kosmos*, 28 September 2019. When asked via email, Polites justified the causes for his anger with the following

statement: "Anger because it's about haves and have nots. And it's about a part of Western Sydney that is about status and superficiality. It's about the worst part of working-class communities." Personal correspondence with the author, 25 April 2020.

9 Theory of mind or mind reading is succinctly defined as "the evolved cognitive adaptation that makes us attribute mental states to ourselves and to other people. [...] Mind reading is approximate guessing and imperfect interpretation, most of it taking place below the radar of our consciousness" (Zunshine xi). The author acknowledges elsewhere in the book that mind reading is a misnomer and would be best called "mind misreading" (2) in so far as the interpretation that underlies the attribution is often approximate, if not erroneous altogether.

10 The word object is here to be understood in psychoanalytic terms, namely "something to which a subject relates. This can be a person, a physical thing or a concept." "Object," Changing Minds, http://changingminds.org/disciplines/psychoanalysis/concepts/object.htm (accessed 22 April 2020).

11 I concur with Sue Kim when she says that

> anger also reflects conflicts within a society. As cultural studies teaches us, cultures are not monolithic or homogenous; rather, culture can be the site(s) of ideological contestation, where different value systems, social groups, and material interests vie for dominance. So people may become angry when different rules of different cultural groups conflict with one another, or when cultural rules about fairness or morality contradict with the material limits that society puts on certain individuals.
>
> (2)

12

> To have, to lose, to do and undo, and redo differently, to create, uncreate, recreate indefinitely our relationships with people and things, this is what always seems new and fascinating in the endlessly-renewed games humans play in search of our pleasure, and our self-conquests. Searching also for mastery of the reality of nature, of the society of which the human is always at once contributor and object. It is the free organization of fantasies of his desires that he wants to make a game of, without too much risk, to find his pleasure and to share it with his fellow humans.

Françoise Dolto, *Les étapes majeures de l'enfance* (Paris: Gallimard, 1994), 121. Trans. Carolyne Lee (qtd in Vernay 30).

13 Karl Enenkel and Anita Traninger remind us that Aristotle was conceiving anger as a pleasure and pain dialectics:

> While they may have been contested by later commentators, it is Aristotle's influential definitions, given in the *Nicomachian Ethics* and the *Rhetoric*, that serve as the point of reference for most later developments. Aristotle construes anger as the desire for revenge for a perceived slight (*oligôria*). Conceived thus, anger joins pain and

pleasure together, as it roots in pain suffered, but results in the pleasurable anticipation of sweet revenge.

(2)

14 A literary technique used in drama and derived from Greek tragedies, *reported action* is when characters would report on stage some (usually violent) unstaged deed/episode. This rhetorical trick would help reduce the performance time of plays and lessen the shocking impact of violence on audiences.

15 Her assertion is followed by a fascinating comment on power politics:

> In most cases, the anger of the privileged group is seen as justified, while the anger of a subordinate group is often seen as hysterical, irrational, and/or dangerous. In the West, the differential characterization of anger according to social power has to do with the relationship of the emotion to the feeling person's cognition, reason, or "intellect," which is often linked to the person's body. That is, male anger is more often linked to reason and is not located in his/her body as a kind of neurotic symptom, whereas women's anger is seen as hysterical and located in her instability as a body (e.g., premenstrual syndrome). This pattern is changing, of course, in the context of late capitalism's changing demands for "sensitivity" and "flexibility," indicating again that the constructions of anger, and how those constructions of anger construct us, are always *historical*. For example, the valences of male anger are raced, classed, and sexed: black male rage is seen as just as irrational but more threatening than female anger; working-class male anger tends to be read by the middle class as irrational, ignorant, and/ or threatening; and gay male anger is seen as just as hysterical and physically neurotic as women's.

Works Cited

Alcaro, Antonio, Stefano Carta, and Jaak Panksepp. "The Affective Core of the Self: A Neuro-Archetypal Perspective on the Foundations of Human (and Animal) Subjectivity." *Frontiers in Psychology* 8 (2017): article 1424. https://doi.org/10.3389/fpsyg.2017.01424.

Bartlett, Neil. "*Merciless Gods* review – Christos Tsiolkas's shocking stories of Australian life." *The Guardian* 1 Oct. 2015. www.theguardian.com/books/2015/sep/30/merciless-gods-christos-tsiolkas-review-short-stories-australia.

Enenkel, Karl A.E., and Anita Traninger, eds. *Discourses of Anger in the Early Modern Period*. Leiden: Brill, 2015.

Gildersleeve, Jessica. *Christos Tsiolkas: The Utopian Vision*. Amherst, MA: Cambria P, 2017.

Johnson, Heather Taylor. "Review of '*Merciless Gods by Christos Tsiolkas.*'" *Transnational Literature*, May 2015. https://dspace.flinders.edu.au/xmlui/bitstream/handle/2328/35321/Complete_Reviews_CLW_May_2015.pdf;jsessionid=54DAD85FC3F428CD9502A3DE603D0A24?sequence=1.

Kim, Sue J. *On Anger: Race, Cognition, Narrative*. Texas: U of Texas P, 2013.

Ley, James. "Frequent Coarse Language: *Merciless Gods.*" *Sydney Review of Books* 1 Sept. 2015. https://sydneyreviewofbooks.com/frequent-coarse-language/.

McCann, Andrew. *Christos Tsiolkas and the Fiction of Critique: Politics, Obscenity, Celebrity.* New York, NY: Anthem P, 2015.

Patel, Jainish, and Prittesh Patel. "Consequences of Repression of Emotion: Physical Health, Mental Health and General Well Being." *International Journal of Psychotherapy Practice and Research* 1.3 (2019): 16–21.

Polites, Peter. *The Pillars.* Sydney: Hachette, 2019.

Seltzer, Leon F. "Angry Tears." *Psychology Today*, 29 Apr. 2015. www.psychologytoday.com/au/blog/evolution-the-self/201504/angry-tears>.

Stamocostas, Con. "Peter Polites: 'Mortgage, success, houses, investment. These aren't Greek values.'" *Neo Kosmos*, 28 Sept. 2019. https://neoskosmos.com/en/146861/peter-polites-mortgage-success-houses-investment-these-arent-greek-values/.

Tsiolkas, Christos. *Loaded.* Sydney: Random House, 1995.

———. *Dead Europe.* Sydney: Random House, 2005.

———. *The Slap.* Sydney: Allen & Unwin, 2008.

———. *Barracuda.* Sydney: Allen & Unwin, 2013.

———. *Merciless Gods.* Sydney: Allen & Unwin, 2014.

Vernay, Jean-François. "The Politics of Desire: A Freudian Reading of Christos Tsiolkas's *Dead Europe.*" *The Journal of the European Association of Studies on Australia* 3.2 (2012): 80–89.

———. *The Seduction of Fiction. A Plea for Putting Emotions Back Into Interpretation.* Trans. Carolyne Lee. New York, NY: Palgrave Macmillan, 2016.

Wolke, Dieter, and Suzet Tanya Lereya. "Long-term effects of bullying." *Archives of Disease in Childhood* 100.8 (2015): 879–885.

Zunshine, Lisa. *Getting Inside Your Head: What Cognitive Science Can Tell Us about Popular Culture.* Baltimore, MD: The Johns Hopkins UP, 2012.

8 No Time for Outrage? The Demidenko Affair

Literary Representations, Criticism, and Moral Emotions in *The Hand That Signed the Paper*

Introduction

The general context of Australian literary hoaxes, and more specifically of controversies related to identity legitimacy or identity litigations (see Vernay, *A Brief Take on the Australian Novel* 102–107), is highly relevant to understanding why identity-related moral violations and literary fakes are a vexed issue in contemporary Australia and why the Demidenko affair generated so many hostile comments. This extremely complex case presents itself as an entanglement of historical, moral, and legal violations. Australian lawyer and novelist Helen Darville, who published her novel under an impersonation alias (Helen Demidenko) and who now goes under the name of Helen Dale, was by turns criticized for her plot based on a historically incorrect thesis, her fraudulent impersonation of a Ukrainian writer, for cultural appropriation and, last but not least, for plagiarism. In examining a major controversy that generated heated debates within Australian academia, I will bring under close scrutiny the strong, if not sometimes overriding influence of emotions in literary appreciations.

This chapter will not discuss the literary merit of *The Hand That Signed the Paper* (1994), written in what many commentators saw as "dispassionate prose," but rather the passionate controversy it generated. I will analyze the role of moral emotions (namely anger, disgust, and indignation) and the turmoil these controversies created in critical practice and in literary life. The close examination of the main arguments put forward by the anti-Demidenko critics will bring fruitful discussions on the status of fiction in the aesthetic experience and on emotional involvement. Finally, the exploration of indignation will eventually challenge the judgmental categories into which emotions are traditionally classified and may reveal the surprising virtue of a so-called "negative emotion."

DOI: 10.4324/9781003161455-12

A Controversial Novelist Eliciting Moral Outrage

Winner of the Vogel Literary Award in 1993, a prize that allowed her manuscript to be published, *The Hand That Signed the Paper* was initially published as a fiction piece but was assumed to be highly autobiographical based on the fact that most first novels by authors in their early twenties are (Daniels 4). Peritextual (i.e., the author's note) and epitextual elements (i.e., published interviews, articles, and columns by Helen Demidenko discussing the book), along with some indisputable clues in the initial manuscript (such as the name Demidenko appearing in the text, later to be edited as Kovalenko), brought further evidence that this book was allegedly inspired from a true family story and not intended to be a work born of a pure figment of her imagination. It tells the story of a Brisbane-based girl discovering some dark family history. Her Ukrainian uncle Vitaly Kovalenko has undergone Stalin's purges and state-imposed famine, which led to the destruction of his family and fellow villagers. The 1941 German invasion is an opportunity for him to seek revenge by siding with the Nazis and enlisting in the SS Death Squads to commit the worst atrocities.

By a surprising twist of fate, this Ukrainian-impersonating plagiarist had been given the Miles Franklin Award (Australia's national equivalent of the Booker Prize)[1] and the Australian Literature Society Gold Medal in 1995. This controversy, which was intensified by Gerard Henderson on 27 June,[2] a few days after the novel received its Miles Franklin national accolade, troubled the literary establishment which had praised *The Hand That Signed the Paper* to the skies and lauded its account of migrant experience for injecting fresh blood into contemporary Australian fiction. The quote by Jill Kitson on the back cover of the original 1994 edition, and which was removed a year later in the third edition, read: "A searingly truthful account of terrible wartime deeds that is also an imaginative work of extraordinary redemptive power." The passionate debate immediately divided the literary community into pro-Demidenko (Frank Devine, Dame Leonie Kramer, David Marr, Paddy McGuinness, Peter Kirkpatrick, Barry Oakley, Andrew Riemer, and Gerard Windsor) and anti-Demidenko critics (Pamela Bone, Anthony Daniels, Gerard Henderson, Robert Manne, Sonia Mycak, to name a few). While some critics like Andrew Riemer put forward literary and democratic motives (such as creative license and freedom of speech) in support of this transgressive novel, others, like Robert Manne, felt outraged and responded to this moral violation with a vitriolic critique, judging the book to be "morally and historically shallow, coarse and cold, even technically quite incompetent" (1).

The controversy and ensuing moral condemnation essentially stemmed from the disturbing and dubious contents of the novel deemed to be historically incorrect. Nevertheless, the indignant responses fuelled a heated but healthy democratic debate about authentic authorship, the status of fiction, literary judgment, freedom of speech, not to mention representation rights in relation to ethics.

The literary judges of the Australian Literature Society Gold Medal had cause to regret their daring choice, because accusations of anti-Semitism, usurped identity, and plagiarism were brought against Helen D (standing for Demidenko/Darville/Dale). At first, she enjoyed her impersonation when offering the media and readers a string of clichés intended to pay tribute to her Ukrainian culture. Many surprises were in store for her audience and revelations quickly followed: Australians learnt that anti-Semitic ideas ran through the entire work; that the author's fake identity was based on a pack of lies because, despite her claims, she was not the child of a Ukrainian immigrant but of English migrants Harry and Grace Darville.[3] More seriously, Helen D had to defend herself against accusations of plagiarism when it transpired that she had reproduced extracts from such writers as Thomas Keneally and Robyn Morgan. No matter how difficult it was to dispute these charges, Darville's lawyers managed to pass the borrowed excerpts off as a wide-spread postmodern practice.

Cognitive Literary Studies redefine reading as a sensory affective and kinesic experience that stimulates nearly all of the reader's senses and elicits emotions which are likely to be influenced by education and socio-cultural milieux. While there is evidence that emotions can at times improve the literary comprehension of readers,[4] they can equally obscure it as in the case of disgust, anger, and indignation. Designated as two basic emotions in Paul Ekman's taxonomy, anger and disgust are often amalgamated as forms of indignation when it comes to expressing moral outrage, but they clearly need to be dissociated on a functional level for two main reasons. Moral anger and moral disgust cause starkly contrasted physiologically responses[5] and they have "distinct antecedents and consequences" from a sociofunctional perspective:

> Anger [...] predicts preferences for direct aggression, such as hitting, insulting, or yelling at the moral violator, whereas disgust [...] predicts preferences for indirect aggression, such as socially excluding or spreading negative information about the moral vio-lator [...], potentially as a means for coordinating punishment with other people [...]

(Molho 617)

Interestingly, moralists Robert Manne and Gerard Henderson have eschewed direct confrontation with the moral violator, Helen D, by opting for printed or online expressions of morally condemning discourses as punishment strategies.

In *The Demidenko Debate*, Andrew Riemer has noted the high level of emotional involvement characteristic of anti-Demidenko critics: "Perhaps the most notable element in the many expressions of disapproval the novel provoked has been the passionately rhetorical tone adopted by most of its opponents; the language of dismay, outrage, anger, disgust and invective" (Riemer 227). Helen D, the moral violator, became the target of opprobrious responses and the chief moral violation was the anti-Semitic content of the literary work. Demidenko's *The Hand That Signed the Paper* elicited moral emotions of two different kinds: moral anger and moral disgust. *The Culture of Forgetting: Helen Demidenko and the Holocaust* clearly articulates Robert Manne's moral anger, which essentially comes from the belief that the Jewish community (the in-group with which Manne identifies, given that he was born to parents who were European Jewish refugees) has been done a great injustice which begs to be redressed. Moral disgust would have been felt by Gerard Henderson because the moral violation was not personally relevant to him, but rather to an out-group (namely the Jewish community to which he does not belong).[6] It seems that Gerard Henderson has expressed in "A fraction too much 'faction'" a form of disgust which is less aesthetic (i.e., triggered by sensory perception) than ethical (i.e., based on his personal subjectivity or on some preconceived moral judgment). Even though moral disgust, like core disgust, can also be elicited by written stimuli, Giacomo Rizzolatti's mirror neurons have no part to play in this process (see Gallese and Goldman).

Core disgust[7] and moral disgust share a few commonalities – most importantly, they involve the same brain regions ("particularly the lateral and medial orbitofrontal cortex") – and have distinct mechanisms in the sense that "moral disgust produce[s] greater activity than core disgust in the more evolutionary recent anterior region, which some think is involved in more abstract emotional associations" (Jones 769). According to Jorge Moll and his colleagues,

> Disgust is one prototypic emotion with multiple domains that include viscerosomatic reaction patterns and subjective experiences linked to (a) the sensory properties of a class of natural stimuli, (b) a set of aversive experiences and (c) a unique mode of experiencing morality.
>
> (68)

Through their strong emotional engagement with *The Hand That Signed the Paper*, the anti-Demidenko critics pressing charges of anti-Semitism clearly deny literature's right to represent and fathom a diverse range of moral stances. It might now be worth examining in the light of Anglo-American analytic aesthetics how strong a case these moralists had.

Morality, Ethics, and Representation Rights in a Mimetic Literary Narration

All things considered, Helen D is mainly criticized for the anti-Semitic content that is pervasive in her mimetic literary narration, not so much for the falsification of her ethnic background,[8] nor even for her plagiaristic forays, both of which came later in the discussion as additional offences. In *The Culture of Forgetting*, Robert Manne is indignant that Helen D has revived the revenge-based Jewish–Bolshevik conspiracy (*The Hand That Signed the Paper* (*HTSP*) 2–3, 8–10) by pairing together what he sees as two historically unconnected events. On the one hand, Helen D admits in an author's note that *The Hand That Signed the Paper* is "a work of fiction" (*HTSP* vi), and thereby *ipso facto* implies that she is making a fictive use of literary language. On the other hand, she claims in the same prefatory text, at least in the third edition published in 1995 in which her historical sources were added, that the causal controversial relationship she establishes between the Ukrainian famine in the early 1930s and the Holocaust is based on solid historical foundation. It is noteworthy that contemporary literary critics cognizant with Anglo-American analytic aesthetics would not expect to find accurate representations of history in fiction and would rather subscribe to the Western conception of fiction-making: the novel as an alternative, if not as a substitute to reality; in other words, a mode of representations that generates dreams, fantasies, and illusions. According to French·New Criticism – a.k.a. the Nouvelle Critique – expressed in the works of literary philosophers like Roland Barthes, Michel Foucault, and Maurice Blanchot, the reader has no more of a mission to seek truths in the literary text than the novelist has to expound them. Reducing fictional narratives to a catalogue of counter-truths would be misunderstanding the verbal state of literature. As Peter J. McCormick puts it, "storytelling, unlike lying, is pretending without the intention to deceive, a storytelling more like charades than perjury" (138). Therefore, it would be pointless to make assumptions of truth or untruth with fictional statements or to take these representations to be accurate depictions of reality.

While the role of a professional reader like Andrew Riemer (who had worked as a literary academic) is to uncover and reveal the tricks that helped the author construct the illusion, the role of nonprofessional readers like Robert Manne (a public intellectual whose expertise lies in politics and history) is to be taken in by the illusory representation. While the author labors only to embed the reader in a fictitious reality by way of processes that create plausibility, certain readers are being led astray by taking the fictional narrative literally and sometimes initiating controversies – if not legal disputes – which result from the overlapping of the fictional and actual worlds. Robert Manne's choice of words betrays his mistaking *The Hand That Signed the Paper* for a History dissertation:

> In *The Hand* Helen Demidenko <u>had argued that</u> Ukranians had participated enthusiastically in the Holocaust because of the role Jews had played in the Famine that Stalin had contrived. Her novel pitted the two great tragedies of twentieth-century Ukrainian and Jewish history – the Famine and the Holocaust – against each other. It was not surprising that within days of the Demidenko storm, Ukrainian-Jewish relations in Australia were becoming noticeably tense.
>
> (Manne 75–76, underscoring mine)

By taking Darville's literary representations at face value, it is most likely that Manne has fallen a victim to the referential fallacy (*l'illusion référentielle*).

Unlike journalism and other nonfiction subgenres, heterorepresentational fiction does not purport to be a faithful transcription of reality and fictional characters – even if they are representative of humankind – remain "paper beings" to poach Paul Valéry's phrase. The no-reference theory and the pretense theory of Anglo-American analytic aesthetics both concur with the idea that fiction is to be clearly dissociated from reality. Propounders of the no-reference theory take the language of heterorepresentational fiction to be devoid of extralinguistic reality. If the linguistic sign ordinarily refers to a referent (when something is said, it is effective because it exists or occurs in reality), it is quite another matter in the fictional world where the "reference to an absent referent is characteristic of literary discourse whose referent is *always* imaginary."[9] In other words, heterorepresentational fiction is bereft of extralinguistic referential properties and therefore makes no reference to anything other than itself.[10] As Terry Eagleton has it, the paradox of fiction is that it refers to reality in the act of referring to itself. Like Wittgenstein's forms of life, fictions are self-founding; but this is not to deny that they incorporate aspects of the world around them into their self-making, just as forms of life do.

(Eagleton 138)

In short, we might consider that heterorepresentational fiction does not have extralinguistic referential properties,[11] for even the most accurate depiction of Ukrainian people in *The Hand That Signed the Paper* would be an *intra*linguistic reference[12] to the representation of Ukrainian people as it appears in the eyes of imaginative writer Helen D, and not an *extra*linguistic reference to actual Ukrainian people.

In speech-act theory terminology, novelists are great experts in pretended reference for, in Peter McCormick's words,

> The writer of fiction not only pretends to describe and to assert; he or she pretends to refer because the nature of fictional sentences is such that he or she cannot refer. The writer of a nonfictional work in using nonfictional sentences intends to refer; by contrast, the writer of a fictional work only pretends to refer.
>
> (138)

Therefore, pretended reference is just another way of saying that fiction offers *indirect* or *second-degree* references to reality – the *first-degree* reference being fiction referring to anything else but itself. From a purely literary perspective, both the no-reference theory and the pretense theory would provide no ground for accusing Helen D of revisionism or of anti-Semitism.

Through her multiple breaches of ethics (revisionism, deception, and wrongful appropriation of culture and authorship), Helen D has proven to be of dubious morality on a very personal level. On a literary plane, the Demidenko Affair is irrefutable evidence that creative authors seem to be restricted in their choice of topics, given that some of them might be too sensitive to even find representation in the world of fiction. While Helen D has enjoyed artistic license to some degree and has shown that she can convincingly write about things and conditions that are intrinsically alien to her, some disturbing associations and difficult subject matter still have the power to shock and repel readers by reopening old wounds. The Demidenko scandal just goes to remind us that emotions have a capacity for impacting on mental clarity and perhaps also for clouding literary appreciation.[13]

Indignation: Emotional Involvement in the Literary Aesthetic Experience

In this literary scandal, Helen D has been the subject of passionate disputes that often expressed forms of indignation. As Robert Manne has it, "For quite different reasons several members of the liberal intelligentsia now rose in alarm and indignation" (88). It is noteworthy that moral indignation, which could either be caused by moral anger or moral disgust, is badly thought of, mainly because of the negative emotional valence of this displeasure-giving and resentment-generating antihedonic state. Additionally, it can be used as an emotional weapon associated with ostracism tactics to induce negative feelings of guilt, shame, or embarrassment within the moral violator. In the broader category of the so-called negative feelings such as fear, disgust, and sadness, indignation is part of what Sianne Ngai eponymously identified as "ugly feelings." For good measure, it should be mentioned that indignation can also be felicitous, as it is perceived in philosophy to be a "*morally good* feeling" in many respects.[14] Elizabeth Lane Beardsley sees moral indignation as only motivated by anger, describing the former as "the emotion of anger felt toward X by one whose only reasons for this anger are his belief that X did A and his judgement that A is wrong and was done without excuse" (171). However, indignation is not always caused by moral anger because it can sometimes be derived from moral disgust, as in the case of the Demidenko controversy.

Literature has always been an important vehicle for exploring human concerns by experimenting with counterfactual scenarios, yet some readers – whether professional or nonprofessional – are still expecting fiction to convey some sense of truth or authenticity. The literary aesthetic experience can be defined as the sum of fantasy-generating representations that we read and process into mental constructs that are idiosyncratic and therefore vary from one reader or context to the next.[15] Given that reading is a knowledge-intensive activity and that cognition is emotiogenic (namely, it produces emotions), there can hardly be any literary aesthetic experience without some degree of emotional involvement – even if emotions could potentially be repressed. This is why Robert Manne's feeling of indignation over anti-Semitic depictions in Demidenko's fictitious narrative is perfectly legitimate,[16] all the more so as the depictions of Jewish people in the book are far from flattering and close to being a grotesque form of caricature: "[Ulrike] tells people that [Comrade Zhivkov] is an ugly Jew and no woman will touch him, and that's his problem" (*HTSP* 93); "She does not know who Jewish

Bolsheviks are, only who the Jews are. Her father says they are bad people who steal" (*HTSP* 108). Following Richard Lazarus' work, Jean-Marie Schaeffer observes that although "cognition and emotions form two structurally correlated systems," there are nevertheless precious few situations (namely: intellectualization, the axiological neutrality of scientific investigation, and detachment) in which "it is possible to dissociate cognitive from emotional evaluation."[17] Yet passing dispassionate critical judgment, whose detachment has often been perceived as necessary to remain objective in keeping with the view that emotions and cognition are perceived as two competing systems, is clearly derived from an intellectualizing process whose hermeneutic function is classically likened to a criminal investigation in the fashion of Sherlock Holmes.

In Schaeffer's recapitulating of the negative and positive sides of these two competing systems (133), the optimistic outlook would see cognitive processing as capable of channeling and controlling the irrational responses provoked by emotions. Therefore, a professional reader like a literary critic would not turn indignant at a fictitious story while knowing for a fact that the contents of *The Hand That Signed the Paper* are vain imaginings bereft of documentary value. Yet, it could be the case because, as Jérôme Pelletier has it, fiction and nonfiction authors thrive on our propensity to get emotionally involved with texts – be they fictional or nonfictional.[18] If we are now to consider the pessimistic outlook on the two competing systems that envisage emotions as irrational responses which could alter an individual's cognitive processes, it is legitimate to ask ourselves, in this very instance, whether emotions are immune to rational thinking, as it sometimes happens (see Schaeffer 133). Should we see these professional readers as being subjected to the emotional force of the literary work? In the light of neuroscience breakthroughs, it would be pointless to separate – and even oppose as in the case of these competing systems – cognition and emotions that are so intricately connected that scientists are now referring to our "cognitive-emotional brain."[19]

Intriguingly, the literary depictions in *The Hand That Signed the Paper* which are deemed to be morally evil seem to only disturb historians and cultural commentators who are capable of highlighting the discrepancy between facts and fiction. The comparison that Robert Manne tacitly establishes insidiously places fiction and reality on a par, by giving these two different domains (i.e., the worlds of historical facts and fictional artifacts) the same value (i.e., truthfulness) and the same outcome in which morality plays a part (i.e., public outrage). According to the strong constructivist perspective in which emotions come into existence through the social norms that support it,[20] we could argue that Manne's emotional involvement and activism are to some extent related to his Jewish identity and to the fact that his grandparents were victims of the Holocaust. Given that Manne identifies with the moral views and values of his social group (the Jewish community), his

> emotions, here, would partake of a symbolic process of social coordination [...]. [T]his thesis amounts to saying that, by expressing my feelings, I'm acknowledging my belonging to the group and my endorsement of their norms and values, in so far as I am specifically encouraged and pressured by the group to do so.[21]

In any case, the scandal that ensues from Robert Manne's indignation takes the professional reader by surprise because it is neither inherent to the process of literary reception (how could anyone feel indignant at literary creations based on no extralinguistic reference or on pretended reference?) nor to the aesthetic experience of the literary artwork per se, because reading novels is not meant to elicit indignation. However, indignation is an object-directed emotion like contempt, hatred, and anger (see Schaeffer 120–122), and therefore implies the representation of an object. The Demidenko controversy would tend to back up the claim that "formal objects, unlike material ones, are the likeliest to elicit emotions."[22] Otherwise put, the book itself (i.e., its existence as a material object) is not to be blamed for causing Robert Manne to be indignant. The main cause for indignation lies in Darville's infamous thesis (i.e., the formal object) expounded on earlier in this chapter. The fact that the same formal object commended praise and admiration from many other professional readers attests to the uniqueness of the emotional lives of readers and to how fictional narratives resonate differently with their eclectic audiences.

Does this mean that the book as a material object would elicit no emotion?[23] Or is the book subject to a cluster of emotions generated by the sum of both material and formal objects leading to a situation where one emotion would have the capacity to overpower all others? In which case, would so-called negative emotions systematically win over positive ones? Given time, cognitive science and neuroscience will surely bring answers to these questions.

Conclusion

Through an exploration of indignation related to a major literary controversy impacting on Australia's literary establishment and largely related to anti-Semitic content, professional readers are led to probe the philosophical status of fiction and its interaction with the emotional involvement of readers. This dual fraud, literary and identity, is also incontrovertible proof that emotions influence our decision-taking, be it positively or negatively – thus modulating our final judgment.

If one is to pool all the relevant evidence culled from this chapter, it appears obvious that indignation can be construed as a *pharmakon* in both meanings of the word. It is as much a poison that tends to censor or restrict literary creativity as a remedy of sorts, because its affective role fruitfully investigates the aesthetic experience to the point of promoting an ethical sense of disgust and drawing a line between what is fair and unfair through social judgment, thus implicitly and ultimately agitating for compassion with the victims. And in this particular case, literary victimhood is certainly not under consideration.

Notes

1 Helen Demidenko was awarded the Miles Franklin Award in spite of the almost negligible aspects of Australian life in the story because its action takes place in Russia during World War II.

2 While his opinion piece straightens the historical facts in crisp bullet points, it also contains strong negative judgments ("As a work of fiction (or faction), *The Hand That Signed the Paper* is deeply flawed," "her first novel contains an amoral and historically inaccurate message"), if not a disgust-filled statement indicative of how high the passions were running in this controversy: "*The Hand That Signed the Paper* is a loathsome book."

3 As a medical practitioner, Anthony Daniels subtly presents Helen D as a pathological liar while diplomatically labelling her "a chronic fantasist, a Baroness Munchausen" (6).

4 See Kneepkens and Zwaan for its selective role in helping to discriminate information from context and in channeling the reader's attention. Patrizia Lombardo also notes that

> Emotions influence the rational pattern of decision-making. First, they define the parameters taken into account in any choice; second, they speed up the decision process by reducing the amount of alternatives to those relevant in a given situation. Without emotions decisions would never be taken, and we would linger in the infinite web of parameters and goals before our minds.
>
> (Lombardo 2)

5 "Whereas anger pushes the heart rate up, being viscerally disgusted makes it drop" (Jones 769).

6

> Our results suggest that the emotion elicited by moral violations shifts toward anger when the costs of the violations increase, such as when

the self is directly involved [...]. Especially in the case of moral offences that are not personally relevant and in the case of morally ambiguous acts, disgust may serve to signal condemnation and facilitate taking of sides, while reducing the risk of escalating conflict.

(Molho 617)

7 At its most visceral level, core disgust could be defined along the lines of evolutionary theory as an emotional response born of the need to protect the human species from food contamination and poisoning (see Jones 768).

8 In her compelling article, Sonia Mycak argues that the Australian literary establishment did not investigate the imposter's Ukrainian–Australian background or the connections she might have to this hyphenated literary community. Moreover,

no Ukrainian–Australian writers, editors, publishers, literary groups of academics were approached for comment. The voice of the Ukrainian–Australian community was barely heard. One article, written by Monash University's Marko Pavlyshyn, was published in the *Australian*. This was the sole space within the print media the Ukrainian–Australian community was able to negotiate, despite repeated attempts approaching all major newspapers across the country for more than six months.

(127)

9 Here is the full quote:

La plupart du temps d'ailleurs on parle des choses en leur absence plutôt qu'en leur présence. Dire 'l'homme que j'ai rencontré ce matin' c'est renvoyer à un référent in absentia que l'on va s'attacher à 'évoquer', à rendre 'présent' par description définie, détermination, qualification, etc. Ce renvoi à un référent absent est caractéristique du discours littéraire dont le référent est *toujours* imaginaire [...]

(Cordesse 83)

10 Jukka Mikkonen traces the no reference theory to "Gottlob Frege's philosophy of language" (4–5).

11

In sum, it makes little sense to claim that fictions do not have referential properties (truth values) just because they are not asserted. We have, after all, no trouble recognizing something to be false in our world – for instance, that there is no such thing as the Library of Babel or the Lottery of Babylon – but true in the story, as in Borges's eponymous tales.

(Swirski 83)

12 With his provocative phrase "fictional truth" – a core problem in analytic aesthetics – Michael Riffaterre endorses the idea that there is intralinguistic referentiality but no extralinguistic referentiality because signs make reference within the structure of signs:

> In fact, *exterior referentiality is but an illusion*, for signs or sign systems refer to other sign systems: verbal representations in the text refer to verbal givens borrowed from the sociolect, but such verbal givens are actually present in the text, explicitly or implicitly, as presuppositions.
>
> (Riffaterre 3)

13

> The extent to which emotional upsets can interfere with mental life is no news to teachers. Students who are anxious, angry, or depressed don't learn; people who are caught in these states do not take in information efficiently or deal with it well. [...] powerful negative emotions twist attention toward their own preoccupations, interfering with the attempt to focus elsewhere. Indeed, one of the signs that feelings have veered over the line into the pathological is that they are so intrusive they overwhelm all other thought, continually sabotaging attempts to pay attention to whatever other task is at hand.
>
> (Goleman 78–79)

The view that emotions would affect reason and cognition was already expressed almost 50 years earlier by W.K. Wimsatt Jr. and M.C. Beardsley in "The Affective Fallacy": "Emotion, it is true, has a well-known capacity to fortify opinion, to inflame cognition, and to grow upon itself in surprising proportions to grains of reason" (38).

14

> [Indignation] is judged to be a *morally good* feeling that we ought morally to feel, and having a disposition to feel indignant feeling is conceived to be a constituent, and key constituent, of moral goodness, of moral worth. A disposition to indignant feeling is also perceived as related inextricably to other important constituents of moral goodness: Feeling (other-regarding) feelings of sympathetic concern for others, and in general, of a special sensitivity to matters of morals. Feeling (self-regarding) feelings of indignation over wrongs we ourselves suffer is central to a proper sense of dignity and self-respect. And feeling (self-reflexive) feelings of indignation over wrongs we ourselves commit is just the passional side of a developed sense of personal integrity and moral responsibility.
>
> (Neblett 139)

15

> Emotions are moulded into widely divergent convictions, action tendencies and normative judgements by individual reflection as well as by the less transparent forces that shape cultural change. Among those forces is the power of words: conversation, debate, rhetoric and argument, all of which are bathed in passion, but all of which still allow for rational debate, providing we are willing to engage in it.
>
> (de Sousa 20)

16 As David Bleich has it:

> The implication is that no matter who makes the critical judgement –
> no matter how impeccable his reputation for 'objectivity' – there is
> an unarticulated emotional basis for a judgement, a basis that would
> be sought by those sufficiently motivated to weaken the judgement's
> status of objectivity. For this reason, it is not unreasonable to assume
> an emotional basis for any critical statement of meaning.
>
> (30)

17 "[...] la cognition et les émotions forment deux systèmes structurellement
corrélés"; "[...] il est possible de dissocier l'évaluation cognitive de
l'évaluation émotive" (Schaeffer 141).

18
> Les auteurs de fiction, comme les auteurs de biographie ou
> de textes historiques, exploitent notre disposition à 'résonner'
> émotionnellement. Il incombe alors au lecteur ou au spectateur d'y
> prendre garde afin de distinguer, par lui-même, les récits de fiction
> des autres types de récit.
>
> (Pelletier 52)

19
> The available research clearly points to a bidirectional rather than a
> unidirectional link between affects and cognition. There is much evi-
> dence for affects influencing attention, memory, thinking, associations
> and judgements ... Equally, however, cognitive processes are integral
> to the elicitation of affective states, as people's appraisal of situational
> information activates appropriate emotional responses.
>
> (Forgas 6)

20 Original text: "les émotions n'ont de réalité qu'en fonction des normes
sociales qui soutiennent leur existence." As opposed to a weak constructivist perspective that would see emotions as playing a transitory social role
("l'émotion est avant tout un rôle social transitoire") (Lepine 141).

21
> L'expression des émotions, ici, relèverait donc d'un processus
> symbolique de coordination sociale [...] [C]ette thèse reviendrait à
> dire, en manifestant mes sentiments, je manifeste mon appartenance
> au groupe, mon adhésion à ses normes et ses valeurs, dans la mesure
> exacte où j'y suis incité et pressé par le groupe.
>
> (Lepine 140–141)

22 "ce sont les objets formels qui déclenchent les émotions davantage que les
objets particuliers" (Lepine 150).

23 The answer to this question can be found in chapter 2 of *La séduction de la
fiction* (Paris: Hermann, 2019), 33–53.

Works Cited

Beardsley, Elizabeth Lane. "Moral Disapproval and Moral Indignation." *Philosophy and Phenomenological Research* 31.2 (1970): 161–176.

Bleich, David. "Emotional Origins of Literary Meaning." *College English* 31.1 (1969): 30–40.

Cordesse, Gérard, Gérard Lebas, and Yves Le Pellec. *Langages littéraires.* Toulouse: Presses Universitaires du Mirail, 1991.

Daniels, Anthony. "Literary Victimhood." *The New Criterion* 18.1 (1999): 4–9.

Eagleton, Terry. *The Event of Literature.* New Haven/London: Yale UP, 2012.

Forgas, Joseph P., ed. *Feeling and Thinking: the Role of Affect in Social Cognition.* Cambridge: Cambridge UP, 2001.

Gallese, Vittorio, and Alvin I. Goldman. "Mirror Neurons and the Simulation Theory." *Trends in Cognitive Sciences* 2 (1998): 493–501.

Goleman, Daniel. *Emotional Intelligence.* London: Bloomsbury, 1996.

Henderson, Gerard. "A fraction too much 'faction.'" *The Age* 27 Jun. 1995: 15.

Jones, Dan. "The Depths of Disgust." *Nature* 447 (2007): 768–771.

Kneepkens, E.W.E.M., and Rolf A. Zwaan. "Emotions and Literary Text Comprehension." *Poetics* 23 (1994): 125–138.

Lazarus, Richard. "Thoughts on the Relations Between Emotion and Cognition." *American Psychologist* 37.9 (1982): 1019–1924.

Lepine, Samuel. "La construction sociale des émotions: enjeux conceptuels et limites d'une hypothèse." *Klesis – Revue philosophique* 23 (2012): 134–165.

Lombardo, Patrizia. "Introduction: The Intelligence of the Heart." *Critical Quaterly* 50.4 (2008): 1–11.

Manne, Robert. *The Culture of Forgetting: Helen Demidenko and the Holocaust.* Melbourne: Text Publishing, 1996.

McCormick, Peter. *Fictions, Philosophies and the Problems of Poetics.* Ithaca/London: Cornell UP, 1988.

Mikkonen, Jukka. "The Realistic Fallacy, or: The Conception of Literary Narrative Fiction Analytic Aesthetics." *Studia Philosophica Estonica* 2.1 (2009): 1–18.

Molho, Catherine, Joshua M. Tybur, Ezgi Güler, Daniel Balliet, and Wilhelm Hofmann. "Disgust and Anger Relate to Different Aggressive Responses to Moral Violations." *Psychological Science* 28.5 (2017): 609–619.

Moll, Jorge, Ricardo Oliveira-Souza, Fernanda Tovar Moll, Fátima Azevedo Ignácio, Ivan Bramati, Egas Caparelli-Dáquer, and Paul Eslinger. "The Moral Affiliations of Disgust: A Functional MRI Study." *Cognitive and Behavioral Neurology* 18.1 (2015): 68–78.

Mycak, Sonia. "Demidenko/Darville: A Ukrainian–Australian Point of View." *Australian Literary Studies* 21.1 (2004): 111–133.

Neblett, William. "Indignation: A Case Study in the Role of Feelings in Morals." *Metaphilosophy* 10.2 (1979): 139–152.

Ngai, Sianne. *Ugly Feelings.* Cambridge, MA: Harvard UP, 2005.

Pelletier, Jérôme. "Deux conceptions de l'interprétation des récits de fiction." *Philosophiques* 32.1 (2005): 39–54.

Riffaterre, Michael. *Fictional Truth*. Baltimore, MD: Johns Hopkins UP, 1990.

Riemer, Andrew. *The Demidenko Debate*. St Leonards: Allen and Unwin, 1996.

Schaeffer, Jean-Marie. *L'expérience esthétique*. Paris: Gallimard, 2015.

Sousa (de), Ronald. "Really, What Else Is There? Emotions, Value and Morality." *Critical Quarterly* 50.4 (2008): 12–23.

Swirski, Peter. *Literature, Analytically Speaking: Explorations in the Theory of Interpretation, Analytic Aesthetics and Evolution*. Austin: U of Texas P, 2010.

Vernay, Jean-François. *A Brief Take on the Australian Novel*. Trans. Marie Ramsland. Adelaide: Wakefield P, 2016.

———. *La séduction de la fiction*. Paris: Hermann, 2019.

Wimsatt, William K. Jr., and Monroe C. Beardsley. "The Affective Fallacy." *The Sewanee Review* 57.1 (1949): 31–55.

Selective Bibliography

Fiction and nonfiction

Atkinson, Meera Anne. *Traumata*. U of Queensland P, 2018.

Bennett, John. "Getting Emotional." *Five Bells*, 10.1 (2002–2003): 13–16.

Black, Katrina. *Distorted Reflections, Misconceptions*. Austed Publishing, 1992. 43–54.

Brooker, Sarah. *My Lucky Stroke*. Affirm Press, 2020.

Bryden, Christine. *Unlocking My Brain: Through the Labyrinth of Acquired Brain Injury*. Ventura P, 2014.

Carmody, Isobelle. *The Obernewtyn Chronicles*. Puffin, 1987.

Caswell, Brian. *Cage of Butterflies*. U of Queensland P, 2018.

Durham, Christine. *Doing Up Buttons*. Penguin, 1997.

Egan, Greg. *Quarantine*. Legend, 1992.

———. *Teranesia*. Gollancz, 1999.

Gibbins, Ian. "Lessons in Neuroscience." *Urban Biology*. Wakefield Press/ Friendly Street Poets, 2012. 66–68.

———. "cataplexy." *e•ratio*, 21 (2015): www.eratiopostmodernpoetry.com/ issue21_Gibbins.html.

———. "No Glutamate." *Island*, 147 (2016): 55.

———. "entorhinal." *Rabbit*, 17, *Geography* (2016): 60–66.

Jordan, Toni. *Addition*. Text Publishing, 2008.

Lawson, Chris. *Written in Blood*. MirrorDanse Books, 2003.

Lilley, Rozanna. *Do Oysters Get Bored? A Curious Life*. U of Western Australia Publishing, 2018.

McCullough, Colleen. *On, Off*. HarperCollins, 2005.

McFarlane, Fiona. *The Night Guest*. Penguin, 2013.

Meyer, Angela. *A Superior Spectre*. Ventura P, 2018.

Prendergast, Julia. *The Earth Does Not Get Fat*. U of Western Australia Publishing, 2018.

———. "Like Clay." *Double Dialogues*, 19, *The Era of Brokenness* (2018): www. doubledialogues.com/article/like-clay/.

———. "Much of a Muchness." *TEXT: The Journal of Writing and Writing Courses. Peripheral Visions: Special Issues Series*, 57 (2019); www.textjournal. com.au/speciss/issue57/Prendergast.pdf.

Redhouse, Nicola. *Unlike the Heart: A Memoir of Brain and Mind.* U of Queensland P, 2019.

Robertson, Rachel. *Reaching One Thousand: A Story of Love, Motherhood and Autism.* Black Inc., 2012.

Roland, David. *How I Rescued my Brain.* Scribe, 2014.

Salom, Philip. "The Man Who Mistook His Wife for a Hat." *Feeding the Ghost.* Penguin, 1993, pp. 3–4.

———. "Elegy for My Father," *New and Selected Poems.* Fremantle Arts Centre P, 1998. 258–263.

———. "Acupuncturist: Under the Needles," *New and Selected Poems.* Fremantle Arts Centre P, 1998. 264–266.

———. "The Man with a Shattered World," *Alterworld.* Puncher & Wattmann, 2015. 177–181.

Simsion, Graeme. *The Rosie Project.* Text Publishing, 2013.

———. *The Rosie Effect.* Text Publishing, 2014.

———. *The Rosie Result.* Text Publishing, 2019.

Valentish, Jenny. *Woman of Substances: A Journey into Addiction and* Treatment. Black Inc., 2017.

Vallence, Sarah. *Prognosis: A Memoir of My Brain.* Little A, 2019.

Woolfe, Sue. *The Secret Cure.* Pan MacMillan Australia, 2003.

———. *The Mystery of The Cleaning Lady: A Writer Looks at Creativity and Neuroscience.* UWAP, 2007.

Scholarship

Atkinson, Meera Anne. *The Poetics of Transgenerational Trauma.* Bloomsbury, 2017.

Britten, Adrielle. "The Family and Adolescent Wellbeing: Alternative Models of Adolescent Growth in the Novels of Judith Clarke." *International Research in Children's Literature,* 7.2 (2014): 165–179.

———. "A Feeling Connection: Embodied Flourishing as Represented in Contemporary Picturebooks." *The Embodied Child: Readings in Children's Literature and Culture,* edited by Roxanne Harde and Lydia Kokkola. Routledge, 2018. 161–174.

Brophy, Kevin. *Patterns of Creativity. Investigations into the Sources and Methods of Creativity.* Rodopi, 2009.

———. "The Poet and the Criminal: Dreams, Neuroscience and a Peculiar Way of Thinking." *TEXT,* 18.2 (2014): www.textjournal.com.au/oct14/brophy.htm.

Brophy, Kevin, and Sue Woolfe. "Talking about Creativity and Neuroscience." *Island,* 111 (2007): 8–17.

Brydon, Diana. "Experimental Writing and Reading across Borders in Decolonizing Contexts." *ARIEL: A Review of International English Literature,* 47.1–2 (2016): 27–58.

Clarke, Robert. "Intimate Strangers: Contemporary Australian Travel Writing and the Semiotics of Empathy." *Journal of Australian Studies,* 85 (2005): 69–81.

Dalziell, Rosamund. *Shameful Autobiographies: Shame in Contemporary Australian Autobiographies and Culture.* Melbourne UP, 1999.

Denham, Ben. "Difficult Sense: The Neuro-Physical Dimensions of the Act of Reading." *Literature and Sensation*, edited by Anthony Uhlmann, Helen Groth, Paul Sheehan, and Stephen McLaren. Cambridge Scholars Publishing, 2009. 112–121.

Gandolfo, Enza. "Take a Walk in Their Shoes: Empathy and Emotion in the Writing Process." *TEXT: The Journal of Writing and Writing Courses*, 18.1 (2014): www.textjournal.com.au/april14/gandolfo.htm

Gildersleeve, Jessica. *Christos Tsiolkas: The Utopian Vision.* Cambria P, 2017.

Giles, Fiona. "Milkbrain: Writing the Cognitive Body." *Australian Humanities Review*, 43 (2007): http://australianhumanitiesreview.org/2007/12/01/milkbrain-writing-the-cognitive-body/.

Hayles, Katherine. "Greg Egan's *Quarantine* and *Teranesia*: Contributions to the Millennial Reassessment of Consciousness and the Cognitive Nonconscious." *Science Fiction Studies*, 42.1 (2015): 56–77.

Heister, Hilmar. "Empathy and the Sympathetic Imagination in the Fiction of JM Coetzee." *Media Tropes*, 4.2 (2014): 98–113.

Kimberley, Maree. "Neuroscience and Young Adult Fiction: A Recipe for Trouble." *M/C Journal*, 14.3 (2011): www.journal.media-culture.org.au/index.php/mcjournal/article/view/371

Mudiyanselage, Kumarasinghe Dissanayake. "Encouraging Empathy through Picture Books about Migration." *Picture Books and Beyond*, edited by Kerry Mallan. Primary English Teaching Association Australia, 2014. 75–91.

Mundell, Meg. "Crafting 'Literary Sense of Place': The Generative Work of Literary Place-Making." *JASAL*, 18.1 (2018): https://openjournals.library.sydney.edu.au/index.php/JASAL/article/viewFile/12375/11762.

Newton, Pamela. "Beyond the Sensation Novel: Social Crime Fiction and Qualia of the Real World." *Literature and Sensation*, edited by Anthony Uhlmann, Helen Groth, Paul Sheehan, and Stephen McLaren. Cambridge Scholars Publishing, 2009. 34–49.

Pettitt, Joanne. "On Blends and Abstractions: Children's Literature and the Mechanisms of Holocaust Representation." *International Research in Children's Literature*, 7.2 (2014): 152–164.

Prendergast, Julia. "Grinding the Moor – Ideasthesia and Narrative." *New Writing*, 15.4 (2018): 416–432.

———. "Narrative and the Unthought Known: The Immaterial Intelligence of Form." *TEXT*, 23.1 (2019): www.textjournal.com.au/april19/prendergast.htm.

———. "Ideasthetic imagining – Patterns and deviations in affective immersion." *New Writing: The International Journal for the Practice and Theory of Creative Writing*, 2020: www.tandfonline.com/doi/abs/10.1080/14790726.2019.1709508

Reeve, Victoria. "Emotion and Narratives of Heartland: Kim Scott's *Benang* and Peter Carey's *Jack Maggs*." *JASAL*, 12.3 (2013): https://openjournals.library.sydney.edu.au/index.php/JASAL/article/view/9830/9718

Robertson, Rachel. "'Driven by Tens': Obsession and Cognitive Difference in Toni Jordan's Romantic Comedy *Addition*." *Australasian Journal of Popular Culture*, 3.3 (2014): 311–320.

Rubik, Margarete. "Provocative and Unforgettable: Peter Carey's Short Fiction." *European Journal of English Studies*, 9.2 (2005): 169–184.

Spencer, Beth. *The Body as Fiction/Fiction as a Way of Thinking*. Unpublished PhD dissertation. University of Ballarat, 2006.

———. "A Response to Fiona Giles, 'Milkbrain: Writing the Cognitive Body.'" *Australian Humanities Review*, 43 (2007): http://australianhumanitiesreview. org/2007/12/01/a-response-to-fiona-giles-milkbrain-writing-the-cognitive-body/.

Stasny, Angélique. "Settler–Indigenous Relationships and the Emotional Regime of Empathy in Australian History School Textbooks in Times of Reconciliation." *Emotion, Affective Practices, and the Past in the Present*, edited by Laurajane Smith, Margaret Wetherell, and Gary Campbell. Routledge, 2018. 246–264.

Stephens, John. "Writing *by* Children, Writing *for* Children: Schema Theory, Narrative Discourse and Ideology." *Crossing the Boundaries*, edited by Michèle Anstey and Geoff Bull. Pearson Education, 2002. 237–248.

———. "Affective Strategies, Emotion Schemas, and Empathic Endings: Selkie Girls and a Critical Odyssey." *Explorations into Children's Literature*, 23.1 (2015): 17–33.

———. "Picturebooks and Ideology." *The Routledge Companion to Picturebooks*, edited by Bettina Kümmerling-Meibauer. Routledge (2017): 137–145.

Takolander, Maria. "After Romanticism, Psychoanalysis and Postmodernism: New Paradigms for Theorising Creativity." *TEXT*, 18.2 (2014): www. textjournal.com.au/oct14/takolander.htm.

———. "Dissanayake's 'Motherese' and Poetic Praxis: Theorising Emotion and Inarticulacy." *Axon*, 4.1 (2014): www.axonjournal.com.au/issue-6/ dissanayake's-'motherese'-and-poetic-praxis.

———. "A Dark/Inscrutable Workmanship: Shining a 'Scientific' Light on Emotion and Poiesis." *Axon* Capsule, 1 (2015): www.axonjournal.com.au/ issue-c1/darkinscrutable-workmanship.

———. "From the "Mad" Poet to the 'Embodied' Poet: Reconceptualising Creativity through Cognitive Science Paradigms." *TEXT*, 19.2 (2015): www. textjournal.com.au/oct15/takolander.htm.

Thomas, Diana Mary Eva. *Textiles in Text: Synaesthesia, Metaphor and Affect in Fiction*. Cambridge Scholars Publishing, 2017.

Vernay, Jean-François. "Forever in the Postcolonial Process of Growing Up: Change and Changelessness in Christopher Koch's Bildungsroman – Inspired Novels." *The Journal of the European Association of Studies on Australia*, 10.1 (2019): www.australianstudies.eu/?p=1344.

———. "Towards a New Direction in Contemporary Criticism: Cognitive Australian Literary Studies." *The Routledge Companion to Australian Literature*, edited by Jessica Gildersleeve. Routledge, 2020. 116–122.

———. *Neurocognitive Interpretations of Australian Literature: Criticism in the Age of Neuroawareness*. Routledge, 2021.

————. (ed.). *The Rise of the Australian Neurohumanities: Conversations Between Neurocognitive Research and Australian Literature* (New York: Routledge, 2021).

Wentworth, Isabelle. "Home Time: A Cognitive Inquiry into Lisa Gorton's The Life of Houses." *Journal of Literary Semantics*, 50.2, 2021, (forthcoming).

Research theses

Harris, David Sydney. *Contemporary Australian Novels and Crises of Ecologies.* Unpublished PhD dissertation. Deakin University, 2017.

Heister, Hilmar. *The Sympathetic Imagination in the Novels of J.M.Coetzee: Empathy and Mirror Neurons in Literature.* Unpublished PhD dissertation. Humboldt University of Berlin, 2015.

Klein, Dorothee. *The Poetics and Politics of Relationality in Contemporary Australian Aboriginal Fiction.* Unpublished PhD dissertation. University of Stuttgart, 2019.

Mudiyanselage, Kumarasinghe Dissanayake. *The Role of Picture Books in Developing an Empathic Response Towards Cultural Difference.* Unpublished PhD dissertation. Queensland University of Technology, 2016.

Smith, Yvonne Joy. *Brightness Under Our Shoes: The Redress of the Poetic Imagination in the Poetry and Prose of David Malouf: 1960–1982.* PhD dissertation. University of Sydney, 2008.

Spencer, Beth. *The Body as Fiction/ Fiction as a Way of Thinking.* Unpublished PhD dissertation. University of Ballarat, 2006.

Stevens, Christopher David. *Crooked Paths to Insight: The Pragmatic of Loose and Tight Construing.* Unpublished PhD dissertation. University of Wollongong, 1999.

Thomas, Diana Mary Eva. *Textiles in Text: Synaesthesia, Metaphor and Affect in Fiction.* PhD dissertation. University of Wollongong, 2014.

Wentworth, Isabelle. *Catching Time: The Synchrony of Minds, Bodies and Objects in Literature.* PhD dissertation University of New South Wales, 2019.

Journalism

Fitzpatrick, Claire. "Neuroscience in Science Fiction: Brain Augmentation in an Increasingly Futuristic World." *Aurealis*, 105 (2017): 29–32.

Vernay, Jean-François. "Aspies Rule: Empowering Neurodivergence Fiction." Features Section, *The Adelaide Review*, 22 July 2019, 11.

Index

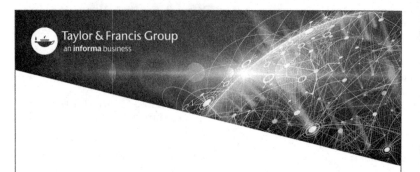

Printed in the United States
by Baker & Taylor Publisher Services